·1977-1990·

Our Lucky Horseshoe

A Memoir of My 13 Years as President of the University of South Carolina

James B. Holderman

Lydia Inglett Ltd. Publishing

Award-winning publishers of elegant books

Our Lucky Horseshoe

A Memoir of My 13 Years as President of the University of South Carolina

ISBN: 978-1-938417-28-3

Published by Lydia Inglett Ltd. Publishing
www.lydiainglett.com
www.starbooks.biz
301 Central Ave. #181 Hilton Head Island, SC 29926
info@starbooks.biz

For my ten grandchildren, and their grandmother, "Mimi,"
Carolyn Rae Meadors Holderman
and our daughters:
Elizabeth Anne Holderman Bradley
Nancy Rae Holderman Smith
Jamie Lynn Holderman Hall

Acknowledgments

Many of those whom I want to acknowledge played a very active role in the story being told through this book. Therefore, I seek to recognize their individual contributions over different periods of time. In virtually every case the relationship is characterized by substantial loyalty and creative directive suggestions. For that I thank them all.

Charles T. "Bud" Ferillo, writer and editor, one whose critical skills are unrivaled and whose many decades of friendship have burst into the formative substantive pages that are this book.

Robert Ariail, internationally acclaimed and recognized editorial cartoonist and editor whose many personal harpoons have done nothing over the years but magnify and strengthen our warm friendship throughout this very book.

The above team of Ferillo and Ariail is an incalculably valuable resource. Singularly they are confounding; together with Bud's insightful attention to prose and Robert's extraordinary sketches, they are the best.

Chris Vlahoplus, a highly trusted and watchful partner for five decades and staunch ally through it all: truly a multi-generational guardian of my interests.

Tommy Stepp, while a relative newcomer (only four decades) to much of the saga of this book, he has always been a vigorous and very wise contributor.

Joseph M. McCulloch Jr., loyal friend and wise attorney, upon whom I seem to have had to rely far too often.

Rachel Haynie, writer and editor, new to this team but not to the practice of authorship.

Alex Haulbrook, trusted tech mainstay whose varied strengths have been critical to the production of this book.

Hannah Haulbrook, editor whose belated addition to this book's development is truly a godsend.

Ginger Wingo Reed, researcher who protectively fought for years as my secretarial guardian, then as one seriously seeking to prepare this book.

Elizabeth West, USC archivist who dug and probed with remarkable success.

Keith McGraw, active participant in and above the fray.

Don Black, the Illinois version of our personal chancellor of the exchequer and trusted friend for many years.

Lydia Inglett, Publisher whose respected talents have helped put this "baby to bed!"

Please note: while some readers may be inclined to regard this as a fictional piece, my wounds from battle tell me otherwise. The people, the incidents, and the various outcomes are quite real – at least to me. Hopefully you will see and understand the full nature of the victories and the struggles as I have. At the very least it might prove to be a "good read!"

Prologue

"Despite Holderman's very public fall, there were those who adamantly defended his administration and insisted that the 1980s were the best decade in the University's history. His supporters cited unprecedented successes in fund-raising, the manifold increases in scholarships and endowed faculty chairs, the procession of national and international leaders and celebrities who visited the campus, the building of a unified University system, the raising of the University's international profile, and the overall sense of enthusiasm and confidence Holderman brought. He declared that the University of South Carolina could be one of the world's top ten universities. With flash and pomp, he taught the University of South Carolina to believe in itself and raise its aspirations, his defenders argued.

There is no question that James Holderman was a dynamic, controversial figure who elicited intense emotion on the USC campus and in South Carolina. His administration left a lasting impact on the University. Was this merely a gilded decade, or was it a watershed period in which Carolina built the foundation necessary for the institution to join the ranks of the nation's prominent research universities? Whatever the passionate arguments of Holderman's defenders and detractors, it must be remembered that the University of South Carolina was far more than "Jim" Holderman, and that for better or worse, the institution made strides during the 1980s that determined much of the direction it took as it looked toward the twenty-first century."

– Courtesy of Henry Lesesne,
A History of the University of South Carolina 1940-2000.

Introduction

Contemplation about the future with a focus on the past is not uncommon among folks my age. I have been thinking over these past few years about how I'd like to be remembered after my days are done. Now at age 79, I know I can say, without a doubt, that my happiest days were those spent as president of the University of South Carolina from 1977 to 1990.

Over the past two decades, I have drafted two separate manuscripts that covered almost everything from my family history dating back to the covered wagon that brought my ancestors to Illinois from my Southern roots in Virginia generations ago to the difficult years following my presidency. In both, I went into so much detail and evoked so many memories, pleasant and unpleasant, that eventually I gave up on both efforts. It is true that, after the loss of my mother in my middle teens, I had what could be labeled an awkward and confused adolescence. It is also the case that after stepping down from Carolina, Carolyn, my wife of 33 years, and I were divorced. I faced bankruptcy, several failed business ventures, time in federal prison and a number of life-threatening illnesses.

I finally asked myself: would anyone really care about all that personal history and trauma when there is a pretty good story to tell about our years at Carolina? Wouldn't it be far better to share these memories and history of these happier times, the journey we made as a family to establish ourselves and leave behind a record of what we actually accomplished?

So that is what I share in the pages that follow. I hope to shed light on those years when we gave our all to build up the strong multi-campus system, erect important buildings and establish world-class programs on the Columbia campus, increase enrollment and stature throughout the University System, seek private philanthropic and federal government funding as state support for higher education steadily declined, and reposition the University of South Carolina as an academic leader in national and global affairs.

Readily admitting to being a hard-charging leader, I never was a placeholder or caretaker president. I certainly was an agent of change. When Pearl Bailey came to Carolina to accept an honorary degree, she said from the commencement podium: "A man without ambition is dead. A man with ambition and no love is dead. A man with ambition and love for his blessings here on earth

Pedal Pushers And Party Pleasers

University of South Carolina President Dr. James B. Holderman wheels ahead Wednesday with the starting gun of a race between USC sorority sisters. Meanwhile, on the sidelines, student Traci Henderson opens wide for some hosed refreshment offered by fellow student Darci Luker. The annual Sigma Nu Little 500, held on the Columbia USC campus, demonstrates the bicycle racing skills of fraternity brothers and sorority sisters. Proceeds of the event go to the Carolina Childrens Home. (Staff Photo by Maxie Roberts)

... and away we go.

is ever so alive." Dear ole Pearl! What a voice, and what a philosophy of life! Those words were directed at all who were there that day, but I took them to heart for my own mission in life. And still do.

My mission in life, for those 13 years, was to advance the overall quality and perception of the University. My measuring stick for our success in that achievement was the Southern Association of Colleges and Schools (SACS), of which the University became an early member in the 1920s. According to the 1991 decennial evaluation required by SACS, the University of South Carolina had been ranked in 1951 near the bottom of almost every ranking category. The faculty, drawing the lowest salaries in the Southeast, was disgruntled. Students were unhappy with overcrowded dormitories, shabby classrooms and inadequate laboratories. The SACS report continued: "Throughout the 1980s, the University brought many distinguished visitors to the system and promoted international studies. Artists and performers were welcomed. Foreign leaders gathered to meet and discuss the changing world scene."

Accomplishments were myriad and sweeping, reflecting how visions and belief in their possibility can bring about their actualization.

Among the first signal accomplishments was the establishment of the Honors College on the historic Horseshoe, an initiative that had been proposed much earlier by Professor Bill Mould, but not acted upon by the University. South Carolina College now ranks number one in the New York Times rating of public honors colleges.

Construction of the $31 million Swearingen Engineering School altered corporate and government perceptions of Carolina and allowed us to weigh in on lucrative research and funding opportunities for which we previously had not been a contender. Without this state-of-the-art facility in place, we might have missed creation of the National Energy Center.

The opening of the $17 million Koger Center renewed our civic vows with our host city, Columbia, and the surrounding metropolitan community, and continues to enable us to attract stellar cultural programming.

The elevation of our Masters in Business degree to *U.S. News and World Report's* #1 ranking, along with completion of construction of the Close-Hipp Business School, gave Carolina viability in arenas that earlier had not taken us seriously.

In unifying our nine-campus system, the sum of the parts became much greater, and the University was not the only benefactor. The status of the faculty and staff, as well as the towns and cities of each campus, were also strengthened system-wide.

The establishment of the James F. Byrnes International Center allowed us to pay tribute to one of South Carolina's greatest statesmen who served as United States Secretary of State in the post-WWII era and also as U.S. Senator and Governor of South Carolina and Associate Justice of the U.S. Supreme Court. Having that institution-within-an-institution thrust us forward as host of conferences convening Caribbean leaders in 1984 as well as numerous other conferences over the years. Our initiatives gained us two visits by President Ronald Reagan in one year, and two by George H.W. Bush, the first during his vice presidency, and then again as U.S. President. For that second visit, First Lady Barbara Bush accompanied him. Both received honorary doctorates from USC.

Our establishment, protection and encouraged growth of the new school of medicine opening in 1977, my first year at Carolina, surmounted many detractors, principally those led by former Governor James B. Edwards, who later became President of the Medical University of South Carolina in Charleston.

The gift of Movietone News footage brought us to the attention of factions that otherwise would not have noticed us, and continues to bring the University to the minds, desktops and proposals of researchers throughout the world.

Acquisition of land was a tangible element in achievements during my administration. Bulldozers and cranes on the scene would be idle today if not for the purchase of property that now is a partial component of the present Greek Village.

We greatly improved our academic standings and established the University as a center of international business, research and diplomacy. Then, just as you'd think, all measures of enrollment throughout the entire System reached all-time highs.

Upon arriving in 1977, we discovered serious organizational problems among the athletic programs. I found we had three quasi-independent athletic directors, each coaching a major sport. However, a single athletic director reporting to the President was strongly recommended – if not required. So, in order to avoid possible problems with the NCAA and any limitations on our possibility of conference memberships, I determined to centralize our athletics department and accomplish the objective of making us fully eligible to whatever considerations we could earn. We had one devil of a fight over that, as each affected party had legions of fans, but we got it done, and the University is the better for it. Membership in the SEC is one major result.

Before my departure, I visited every one of the member campuses in the SEC to indicate our interest in Carolina's possible membership. I heard from a variety of sources that the University of California President Clark Kerr had philosophically observed that "it takes only three things to be a successful college president: parking for the faculty; football for the alumni; and sex for the students." I frequently considered one out of three wasn't bad!

A major need of the University when I arrived was to improve its endowment of only $2.5 million. Annual private giving totaled $1.5 million. In my last full year as president, the endowment surpassed $50 million, and annual private giving exceeded $22.5 million. The number of endowed chaired professorships increased from 19 to more than 100.

In 1981, an old friend, Novice Fawcett, with whom I had worked on a Lilly Endowment-funded panel studying university governance, nominated me for the presidency of Ohio State University. I was serving as Vice President for Education at Lilly when I first became acquainted with Fawcett. When I learned I might be offered the post, I felt that I owed more time to Carolina; my family seemed to be happy and very comfortable here.

The timing paralleled a plan that several campus departments had in the works: to host an international conference of Caribbean leaders that drew the participation of President Reagan in 1984. Because we were launching more and more programs of global significance, attracting more funding, faculty endowments and international recognition, I waved off any interest and avoided having to accept or decline the presidency of OSU. I admit, however, the appeal of returning to the Midwest where I grew up and was educated was strong. The decision was a tough one. My name did reach the media during OSU's search process.

Reporting in the *Columbus Dispatch* on May 29, 1981, staff reporter Gary Keifer wrote these observations of my efforts at Carolina up to that time: "Associates say Holderman's high profile has in turn helped to bring a new visibility to the University of South Carolina … but they also say something else. They don't want him to leave. In fact, a team from the Southern Accreditation Association, visiting Columbia in April to check on its standards and operations, noted in its report that 'a state of euphoria' existed there. Holderman runs his operation on a tight schedule, often setting out by 7:00 a.m. to walk the short distance from his official President's House to his office … on many days, he doesn't make the return trip until 11:00 p.m., or later, after a day crammed with meetings, receptions, lunches or travel."

Keifer's news piece continued: "Holderman generally is credited with helping to put scholarship and research back into the spotlight at South Carolina. … "

That is how I feel most of my 13 years at the helm of Carolina went for me – except for the skirmishes with scattered local media and legislative critics over what they described as "lavish overspending" in my fund-raising role and my reluctance to share what I believed was private information with the media.

You can be sure that my last year took a toll on all of us, and I knew when it was time to throw in the towel. On May 30, 1990, I met with Mike Mungo, board chairman, at his church and handed him my letter of resignation. Our perfunctory meeting took no more than 10 minutes.

Then I went to the Horseshoe to make a short statement to the media, with Carolyn at my side. "For my whole family, this has been more than a job – it has been a total commitment. We are grateful for the tremendous friendships and opportunities it has afforded us. In our collective judgment, we have determined that it is time to pursue new personal and professional challenges."

There were no questions asked, and Carolyn and I walked back to the President's House together, now with only a few days longer to be President and First Lady. Essentially, it was over.

The following day, *The State* newspaper's reporter, Bill Robinson, quoted Steve Benjamin, then USC Student Body President, now Mayor of Columbia: "It is a sad day … a bad day." Bill Bethea, a board member from Hilton Head, was quoted: "The reasons are obvious, aren't they? He has been lambasted and badgered mercilessly for weeks. It gets to a point where you say 'Life is too short!'"

Board member Lily Roland-Hall of Anderson said: "I really think he tried to make us better in spite of ourselves."

Columbia board member William Hubbard, now President of the American Bar Association, made the most powerful statement of all: "He shook our belief that the University would always be mediocre and average. He made us think we could have a national reputation, that we could be Top 10 in anything we set our minds to. He will be remembered as the president who made us believe we could be more than we thought."

There you have it.

I am living out my life with a mix of pride and regret, confident that I gave my best to Carolina and to the state I continue to call home.

My father, with whom I sometimes had what could be called a difficult relationship, as did my brother and sister, wrote me a letter in June 1958 upon my graduation from Denison University in Granville, Ohio. Upon reflection, a good many of his thoughts have been realized in my life: certainly some with real successes and an ample number of disappointments. I recently came upon it again among my personal files and want to share it with this collection of photographs from my years at Carolina. Dad said: "I will wish you enough success to encourage you; enough reverses to keep you humble; enough good fortune to make you grateful; enough opposition to keep you alert and watchful; good health to keep you going; financial success sufficient enough to encourage you and to make you appreciative of what you have, but not to the extent of empowering their importance."

Dad's wishes were very perceptive of my nature, even at that young age, and most prescient for the life I was to lead. Those words of challenge are the best gift he ever bestowed upon me.

I also want to share how my mother, who died from cancer far too young at 49 when I was but sixteen, responded to a question about her philosophy of life. Funny even now, her philosophy is one that I share equally. When she had just learned she was terminally ill, Mom was visited by a spinster-like Sunday school teacher who asked Mom what her philosophy was. Without blinking an eye, and without giving any indication of how tough that question was, being fielded at that precise moment, Mom looked her in the eye and said, with no wavering emotion: "My philosophy of life is quite a simple one. My first name is Helen. My maiden name is Bowker, the initial B, so there it is: Work like Helen B Happy. That's my philosophy of life."

It is mine, too.

Jim

James Bowker Holderman

My father, Judge S. J. Holderman, left, visiting us in Columbia for a reception, talks with Markley Dennis, Chairman of the USC Board of Trustees. They are trying to figure out how to handle me! No luck at that.

Our Home and Family

Beginning late summer 1977, a new First Lady – Carolyn – and three First Daughters – Betsy, Nancy and Jamie – adjusted swiftly and, I must add, graciously to life not only in the South, but also in a Southern fishbowl. Sometimes the demanding lifestyle weighed heavily upon these long-suffering yet dutiful daughters; at the same time, their new home and way of life came with introductions and opportunities to meet and host leaders representing every sphere of humanity. The President's House hosted a perpetual cavalcade of students, faculty, administrators and global citizens. Throughout our time at the University of South Carolina, ours was an open door to prominence.

The dew was still on the roses that May 1978 morning when Father Ted Hesburgh came back into the President's House. In advance of getting ready for the commencement services at which he would be keynote speaker and receive an honorary degree, he and Jamie had gone outside to greet the day. He had blessed the garden and surroundings. Carolyn had breakfast just about ready and I awaited my long-time friend with a glass of orange juice. The exterior of the glass was embellished with the USC logo. He balked when he picked up the glass. "Jim, what are you trying to do to me?" Father Ted asked. You might not know that Father Ted was then the long-serving President of Notre Dame and that the University of Southern California was one of the Catholic institution's fiercest football rivals. He would not have put it past me to prank him by serving him juice in a glass embellished by the logo of his university's staunch rival. "Father Ted," I explained. "The glasses are for this USC, not the one in California." He accepted the explanation a little sheepishly; we all had a good laugh and got ready for commencement, my first since assuming the presidency. Asking him to be the first commencement speaker says a lot about how highly I regarded him and his friendship.

The roles of both host and hostess were requisite to our serving as President of the University of South Carolina, one that Carolyn and I took seriously. The President's House, originally built in 1810 as housing for professors, was rebuilt in 1854 and refur-

Flags flying along the front of the President's House were sometimes the first signs of welcome seen by international guests. This array includes the Papal flag from 1987.

bished often after that. An incident related to Donald and Virginia Russell's refurbishing reveals much about their determination to make the renovations perfect. In a series of unsuccessful attempts to match a paint selection with a paint chip, the University painters finally succumbed and painted the chip. Then they matched without further ado.

Upwards of 20,000 people a year crossed our threshold for meals or receptions. Apparently that still wasn't enough. Occasionally, the uninvited guest showed up. If the front door was left unlocked, it was not unusual for strangers to come in to look around. Even use the bathroom! While our oldest daughter Betsy was studying for exams, she heard unfamiliar voices in the hall. I have learned that she hid under the bed until they left, then tiptoed to the window, hoping to see who it was. The best she could figure it, the gaggle of women were on an unannounced tour. We guessed they "just wanted to see the house."

While observing our first Thanksgiving in the house, we got a pretty good idea why there were two dining rooms. From that holiday on, we considered sharing our family meals in the interior dining room; windows that overlooked the Horseshoe opened the other one to curiosity seekers. We looked up from our plates that November day to see people with their noses nearly pressed to our window. We figured they were out for a Horseshoe stroll, walking off some of the turkey and dressing they had enjoyed earlier.

Another instance in which the public seemed to feel our home was open property involved theft. Our family was away and the campus security force was keeping an eye on things, but they did not detect someone entering and making off with some of Carolyn's costume jewelry. We notified the head of campus security when she noticed items missing after we returned. The culprit was identified, but when law enforcement picked up Auntie Lou's trail, they learned from her neighbors and relatives she had since died, and had been buried, wearing Carolyn's jewelry!

AUNTIE LOU

We greeted our guests by encouraging them to make themselves at home, and usually the overture was taken as sincere. Board Chairman Othniel Wienges and his wife Callie spent the night in the Kennedy bedroom, long before Holiday Inn used as its slogan: Stay with someone you know. As they were leaving, Callie made this Parthian shot over her shoulder: "Oh, by the way, there was no soap in our bathroom." I wish I'd been quick enough to retort:

How proud we were when students chose our daughter Nancy as Homecoming Queen!

"I guess the Pope used it all." After Pope John Paul II left us, we were tempted to refer to that porcelain chamber as the Papal Loo.

On another occasion, Tamie Fraser, wife of Malcolm Fraser, the Prime Minister of Australia, made herself at home by fixing the toilet, too often afflicted with aging problems, in the bathroom adjacent to the Kennedy bedroom, which they were occupying on the visit. "Not to worry; I do it all the time at home," she assured Carolyn in her "Down Under" Aussie accent.

British actor Michael York took the role of handyman while he was a guest. We had a number of guests that particular commencement

weekend. Helen Hayes was there along with Kitty Carlisle Hart, Patricia York, and my wife, all with hairdryers going at once shorted out the electrical system. I was peering into the circuit breaker, trying to figure out what to do when I felt a presence behind me. I turned around and there was Michael, wearing nothing but a towel. He said, "Let me have a look," and in moments he had fixed it. The electricity was restored! Michael, a regular in Hollywood's Musketeers' series, performed well on that day: a champion Musketeer to the rescue!

We had guests who would have been welcome to stay longer, some who overstayed, some who were not invited – and some we never saw.

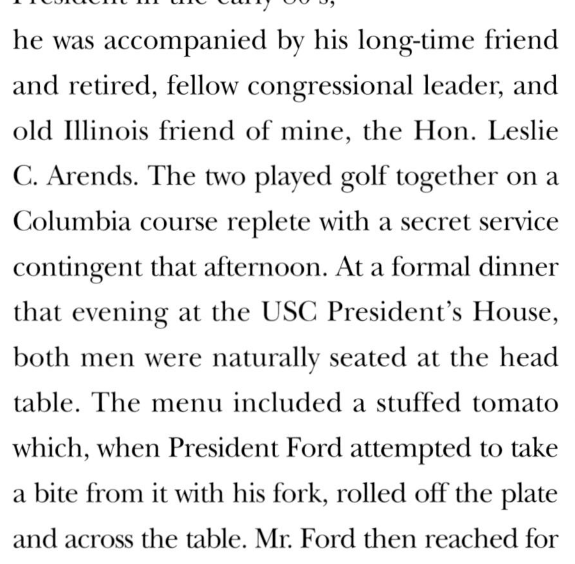

When the Honorable Gerald R. Ford, 38th President of the United States, visited USC as a former President in the early 80's, he was accompanied by his long-time friend and retired, fellow congressional leader, and old Illinois friend of mine, the Hon. Leslie C. Arends. The two played golf together on a Columbia course replete with a secret service contingent that afternoon. At a formal dinner that evening at the USC President's House, both men were naturally seated at the head table. The menu included a stuffed tomato which, when President Ford attempted to take a bite from it with his fork, rolled off the plate and across the table. Mr. Ford then reached for

Our family had the privilege of hosting POTUS to the campus in 1983.

Jamie, our youngest daughter, was a little shy when President Ronald Reagan took her hand in his, but this poised young woman quickly absorbed the rarified moment and made him feel as comfortable as he made her feel.

Nancy, middle daughter, rose graciously to the occasion of welcoming this President, and over the years, many other distinguished guests.

and retrieved it with his open fist, placing it squarely on his plate. After doing so, he pulled his chair back up to the table, bumping the leg nearest his chair. Every water glass on the table shook and sprayed water all over the table. Congressman Arends made the following query of his buddy the former president: "Gerry, you don't seem to be eating out much any more; am I right?" Only he could have asked such a question of the former president!

Rumors that there was a ghost in the President's House had been around for as many administrations as I have connections with. Patricia Moore-Pastides might tell you about the time, fairly recently, when she went up to the McKissick Room to read one night and something – or some specter – kept turning off the light next to the bed. I doubt if anyone in my family would refute its presence. My daughters often reported that the elevator went up and down during the night and, of course, no one was in it. Evidence of a spirited presence could also be found, from time to time, on the third floor. The creaking of a rocking chair could be heard all during the night, and the next morning, the carpet beneath the rockers would be creased, as it would be from the weight of someone sitting and rocking in that chair. Whether incidentally or not, the rocker which is alleged to have rocked on its own originally came west to Illinois from Virginia on a covered wagon by my great great-grandparents in 1831, and then south with us to Carolina in 1977, prompting the question: "Was the chair merely pleased to have finally found its Southern roots?"

A recurring problem during my presidency was the theft of various flags flown off the front of the President's House. No doubt, many of the pranks were rites of passage into fraternities, or just students wanting a South Carolina or University flag. Rarely was an American flag stolen. We never caught a single flag thief! At one point I suggested we have the flag poles

Betsy found meeting dignitaries, such as Henry Kissinger, increasingly natural. Behind Henry is Provost Frank Borkowski.

Jamie greeted former Secretary of State Kissinger with a firm handshake.

wired to give off a low-voltage shock to any trying to take the banners down, but we decided to avoid even more trouble and just replaced them when necessary.

On more than one occasion, Carolyn remarked to me: "We should have the faculty to dinner!" Good idea! But difficult to pull off, at least in a singular event. We began inviting small groups monthly, 40 or 50 faculty members – and spouses – throughout the academic year in a random fashion designed to avoid duplication. The events became a well-received activity with few regrets, but we did hear from faculty members saying they wanted to come again. This was one of Carolyn's many great ideas. She made that initiative work as she did many other things. As I've said repeatedly, she was a first-class First Lady.

At these dinners and receptions, faculty members who seldom had the opportunity to be under the same roof enjoyed camaraderie and felt comfortable enough to speak their minds. It was at one of the early dinners that I heard an English department professor recounting his visit of condolence to Jim Dickey, the very morning his second

On a day in the mid-'80s when Carolyn could not join in saying farewell to our guest, Betsy filled her mother's role in wishing Monsignor Agripino Núñez Collado a safe flight back to the Dominican Republic.

Nancy, Betsy, Mister Rogers and Jamie – in our neighborhood.

wife Maxine passed away. Dickey asked his colleague: "How long do you think I have to wait before I start dating?" By all counts he did not wait for an answer; he must have begun dating that same day because two months later he married Deborah, one of his former students.

Those gatherings were like huge family dinners to me. On a smaller, much more intimate scale, my own family rose to the challenges inherent to the loss of privacy. They created some enduring memories, developed skillsets they have found useful in their lives, and have always made me proud.

When your front yard is the historic Horseshoe, you are nearly compelled to horsing around. My predecessor had issued a prohibition: No Frisbees on the Horseshoe. When I found out about that edict, I ordered 100 garnet Frisbees imprinted with Presidential Platters in black lettering and asked students to distribute them. For some time after that edict was lifted, the airspace on the Horseshoe was filled with flying Frisbees.

For this graduate, a handshake was not nearly warm enough to express my love and congratulations – Jamie was our third and last daughter to graduate from the University of South Carolina.

Lord Peter Carrington chats with Carolyn at dinner.

Carolyn and I go over the European Security Conference schedule at the Russell House with Vice President George H.W. Bush in 1987.

Our Team

Like a saying culled from much earlier days: "One for the money, two for the show, three to get ready, four to go!" Carolina was ready!

The team at the University of South Carolina from 1977 to 1990 was far larger than the relatively few cited by name on these pages. Our growth, new measures of national and international regard and respect would not have happened if the entire university family were anything short of ready, willing and excited about our momentum and improved stature among our peers. Over 125,000 students received degrees in those years; their extraordinarily infectious enthusiasm added immeasurably to Carolina's momentum. All of these constituencies, together, were the Carolina team of that exciting era. It was my personal privilege to be a part of that thrust in those exceptional years.

Late in the eighties while flying home to Columbia from an alumni reception and dinner in the greater Boston area, several of the Carolina system team and I were engaged in a relaxing game of Trivial Pursuit, which we frequent flyers on the University plane often enjoyed. The flight itself seemed quite typical, even relaxing, as we figured we were about halfway home well into the evening. Then, all on board our small plane were jolted by a blasting, commanding voice blared out from our speakers: "IDENTIFY YOURSELF, IMMEDIATELY! IMMEDIATELY!" Even our highly qualified, experienced and generally quite steady chief pilot, Roger Booco, sounded a bit shaken as he responded: "CHARLIE FOXTROT REGISTERED TO THE UNIVERSITY OF SOUTH CAROLINA!" The voice of authority returned and announced: "YOU HAVE ENTERED RESTRICTED AIR SPACE OVER THE WHITE HOUSE AND YOU MUST LEAVE IT IMMEDIATELY OR SERIOUS STEPS WILL BE TAKEN BY AIR TRAFFIC CONTROL!" Our pilot understood precisely what the ground control officer was saying and indicated our intent to comply promptly. The voice from air traffic control returned a moment later and inquired: "YOU SAID YOU ARE REGISTERED TO THE UNIVERSITY OF SOUTH CAROLINA?" Our pilot responded in the affirmative and the air traffic control officer again came back on the air: "WELL, THAT IS A REAL COINCIDENCE – THAT IS WHERE I GRADUATED A FEW YEARS AGO! GOOD LUCK! GET OUT OF HERE RIGHT NOW, AND STAY OUT!" We did just that, thanking the Almighty for our "very lucky" meet-up with an alum of real consequence!

Chris Vlahoplus, who was the nucleus of the Holderman Team that formed incrementally at USC, came with me from the Midwest. Chris and I had already been friends since the 1960s; how fortunate I was that Chris was willing to come with me as I began my presidency here. We met when he was the United Press International (UPI) Bureau Chief in Springfield, Illinois; we became friends and have remained so. He was the heart, mind and vision of my tight-knit team throughout the administration. His starting title was Executive Vice President of Public Affairs. Later on, after George Curry retired, Chris also became Secretary to the Board of Trustees, a post he held through 1987. His service included responsibility for several University foundations. He was the director of the Summitt Fund Campaign: the first and largest capital fund drive in USC history to that day. He left the administration to accept a professorship in the College of Journalism.

Some who, far and away, proved their mettle as essential members of the team were already in place when I arrived late summer, 1977; others came on board along the way.

James Kuhlman had been a student at Northwestern when I was a teaching assistant there during my graduate school days. Low and behold, when I arrived at Carolina, he was already teaching in GINT (Government and International Studies) on the Columbia campus. In 1980, he was named to direct initiatives of the new James F. Byrnes International Center and did an exemplary job there throughout the remainder of my administration.

Johnny Gregory came aboard about midterm. A highly lauded Gamecock football hero, he was a great asset to the University as liaison to the Legislature for more than seven years.

J. McCauley "Mac" Bennett served as Executive Assistant to the President, Assistant Vice President for Administration and Chief of Staff for the Byrnes International Center.

Johnny Gregory, left, and Chris Vlahoplus were essential advisors to our team.

Jake Jennings was another team member with whom I had a lengthy friendship dating back to Illinois. Jake came to USC and was with us as Vice President for Community Affairs for the last five years of my administration.

Steve Beckham, a staff acquisition brought on early in 1977, soon went to Washington, D.C. as our liaison with Congress and is still there doing a splendid job representing the University's interests on Capital Hill.

Tommy Stepp already had given about 25 years of service to the State of South Carolina before he became Vice President for Administration in 1985. As only one facet of his work, he saw to it that the Koger Center advanced – from the pouring of the footings to opening night – and has continued to hear from some of entertainment's most celebrated performers that the Koger Center is one of the best venues, acoustically, in the country. He was the second longest-serving Secretary to the Board of Trustees in the University's history, later joining the Osborne staff and serving as a senior officer in my administration.

Provost Frank Borkowski, at my side, was a critical team member during all of his tenure at Carolina.

"Pete" Stokes, left, with Jake Jennings, right, who had impressed me so greatly in Illinois that I found a position for him here at Carolina. He joined the team in 1985 as Vice President for Community Relations.

In all of his years of service to Carolina and beyond, Tommy Stepp and his wife Sara remain great friends.

Dennis Pruitt became Dean of Students early in the 1980s; he continues now as Vice President for Student Affairs.

Dave Rinker, Vice President for Facilities Planning, had to call me the very morning we were to break ground for the Swearingen Center and tell me he was unsure if we had clear title to the property. A phone call was made to Bob McNair who somehow got that oversight troubleshot just before the bulldozer cranked up that afternoon.

Paul Ward was the University System's Vice President for Legal Affairs between 1979 and 1991. He worked with me at Lilly Endowment in Indiana before coming with me to the University of South Carolina.

Joe McCulloch was an associate attorney working closely with Paul Ward as an outside counsel.

Carl "Pete" Stokes entered law enforcement soon after graduating from Carolina and, after long service to the South Carolina Law Enforcement Division, came home and immediately began serving as Systems Vice President for Law Enforcement and Safety. Under his leadership, the University police and security force were professionalized remarkably. He saw to the provision of personal security through a roster of officers including: Ernie Ellis, Mike Genau, Rick James, Steve Wright and John Bradley.

George Terry, University Archivist, was also Vice Provost and Dean of Libraries.

Carol Benfield, center, a "Jacqueline of all Trades" for all of us in the administration, makes Mahmoud and Yasmina Karem feel right at home at Carolina.

Distinguished Professor of International Studies Charles Kegley, right, welcomes Japanese Ambassador Yoshio Okawara and his wife Mitsuko.

Having Johnny Gregory in my corner always gave me a sense of security. His service to USC resembles his performance on the gridiron: loyal and flawless!

Frank Borkowski, former Chancellor of the University of Indiana at Fort Wayne, was USC's Executive Vice President and Provost for the majority of my tenure.

Jane Jameson was Vice President for Personnel, the first female Vice President in the University's history.

John Duffy, a real long-timer, was Vice President for University Campuses and Continuing Education early in my administration. He later served as Vice Provost and Executive Dean and was instrumental in strengthening the University System.

Robert W. "Pete" Denton served as Vice President for Finance and University Treasurer for the System. A Carolina graduate, he worked his way up in the University financial system and helped manage in times of financial stringency.

Robert J. "Bob" Woody, a prominent Washington attorney, served as the principal counsel for the University in the nation's capital during all of my tenure.

Jonathan Davidson, a former British Foreign Service officer, served from 1981 to 1991 as Special Assistant to the President for International Programs in Washington, D.C.

Pomp and Circumstance

Before being invited to impart words of wisdom and encouragement at commencements and convocations, invitees first had to be relevant to our students. With that component as the vital baseline, we tried to balance the prospective wisdom an invitee might convey with his or her public relations potential. Ceremonies more than several times a year, sometimes as many as eleven, afforded us bountiful opportunities to robe for success. To have our backyard – where convocations were held – or our commencement stage studded with such stellar representatives of government, industry, business, entertainment and sports provided memorable send-offs for our graduates and inspiration for our current students. During my years as President of USC, President Ronald Reagan visited twice and George H. W. Bush visited both as Vice President and President and spoke at the final commencement over which I presided.

Juanita Kreps was Jimmy Carter's pick as his Secretary of Commerce, the first woman – out of 24 – to hold the position. I thought she was the ideal choice for speaker at my inauguration ceremony, in part because student body demographics were tilting: females were outnumbering males for the first time since WWII. My initial connection with her had been through our mutual involvement with the Lilly Endowment. She became the first female director of the New York Stock Exchange. Her being on our campus brought us good media coverage, and her remarks were well received.

Orchestrating President Ronald Reagan's first visit to USC was the White House. President Reagan was coming here to receive an honorary degree – and then to attend an off-campus reception for Strom Thurmond. Prior to the honorary degree ceremony on the Horseshoe, we met the President at McKissick Museum where I gave him a Steuben glass sculpture, Excalibur. He couldn't pull the sword out of the stone. After a couple of tries, he asked me, "Is this a joke?" That exercise seemed to warm him up to being here. Later that same year, a White House aide with connections in Carolina told us we wouldn't be able to get the President back for the Caribbean Conference in the summer of 1984. I demurred, and went right on planning the conference around Reagan. As a result, we soon had more than fifteen Caribbean presidents and prime ministers saying they would come if the President came. Their confirmations that they would participate in the conference sealed the deal: President Reagan did, indeed, come

DISTINGUISHED GUESTS
Commencements, Convocations and Conferences

Salvador Jorgé Blanco, President of the Dominican Republic
Andreas Van Agt, Prime Minister of the Netherlands
Hernandez Colon, Governor of Puerto Rico
Edward Hennessey, Chairman/CEO of Allied Signal
John Clendennin, Chairman/CEO of Bell South,
Chairman of the United States Chamber of Commerce
Joe Riley, Mayor of Charleston, South Carolina
Father Theodore Hesburgh, President of Notre Dame University
Herman Wells, Chancellor of Indiana University
U.S. President Gerald R. Ford
Jody Powell, Press Secretary for U.S. President Jimmy Carter
Jehan Sadat, wife of Egyptian President Anwar Sadat
Yoshio Okawara, Japanese Ambassador to the United States
Sir Oliver Wright, U.K. Ambassador to the United States
Juanita Kreps, U.S. Secretary of Commerce
Ira Koger, Chairman and CEO of Koger Properties
John Swearingen, Chairman/CEO of Standard Oil of Indiana
Peter Hermes, West German Ambassador to the United States
Günther Van Well, West German Ambassador to the United States
Chai Zemin, People's Republic of China Ambassador to the U.S.
Allan Gotlieb, Canadian Ambassador to the United States
Bernardo Sepulveda Amor, Mexican Ambassador to the U.S.
Shintaro Abé, Trade Minister of Japan
Kurt Waldheim, Secretary General of the United Nations
Lord Peter Carrington, Foreign Secretary of the United Kingdom
Malcolm Fraser, Prime Minister of Australia
Armand Hammer, CEO of Occidental Oil
Pearl Bailey, Entertainer
Danny Kaye, Entertainer, Honorary Chairman of UNESCO
Henry Kissinger, U.S. Secretary of State
Jim Brady, Press Secretary to President Ronald Reagan
Bill Cosby, Entertainer
Mister Fred Rogers, Entertainer
Jimmy Stewart, Entertainer
Helen Hayes, Entertainer
Walter Cronkite, Newscaster
Jim Lehrer, Newscaster
Robin MacNeil, Newscaster
Robert Morley, Entertainer
Ron McNair, Astronaut
Lawrence Eagleburger, U.S. Secretary of State
Admiral James Stockdale
Arthur Ashe, Tennis Champion
Reverend Billy Graham, Evangelist
Right Reverend Robert Runcie, Archbishop of Canterbury
Joseph Cardinal Bernardin, Archbishop of Chicago
Michael York, Entertainer
Kitty Carlisle Hart, Entertainer
U.S. Senator Mark Hatfield
Ted Koppel, Newscaster
Alex Haley, Author
John Williams, Conductor and Composer
Carl Sagan, Astronomer
William F. Buckley, Journalist
Lane Kirkland, Labor Leader
Robby Benson, Entertainer
Stanley Donen, Writer and Director
Michael Eisner, Business Leader
Richard Thomas, Entertainer
Cicely Tyson, Entertainer
Macdonald Carey, Entertainer
U.S. President George H.W. Bush
U.S. President Ronald Reagan
Robert Crippen, Astronaut
John Young, Astronaut
Warren Burger, Chief Justice of the United States

back to USC. The White House chose a date for the President's ultimate visit in July of 1984 coinciding with the keynote address of the Democratic National Convention of that year: obviously a different place and agenda.

When Vice President George H.W. Bush addressed a later conference on the future of the Western Community, he began his speech by referring to the previous year's Caribbean conference:

"The University has made Columbia a center of pilgrimages by statesmen … Who knows? One of these days, if this keeps up, America will get its own equivalent of Vienna or Geneva right here in Columbia."

Bush had no idea that plans were being made, even then, to host an International Monetary Fund Conference at the Byrnes International Center that would draw 20 of the nation's leading financial leaders to the University.

Another outstanding role model to speak from our commencement podium was Mark Hatfield, one of the finest leaders in our country during my time at USC. He was a U.S. Senator from Oregon, and his career in public service was exemplary. After graduating from Willamette University, he served in the U.S. Navy in the Pacific Theater during WWII, afterwards went for a Ph.D. in political science from Stanford University, and later returned to Willamette as a professor of political science. While still teaching at Willamette, he was elected to both bodies of the Oregon legislature, then a

When former president Gerald R. Ford visited us, he attended a reception at the President's House. President Ford was approached and punched in the stomach by legendary retired Clemson Athletic Director, Frank Howard. As he punched the former President, Coach Howard was heard to say, "Oh, yeah! You played football too often without a helmet." While the President seemed to take it in stride, accompanying Secret Service appeared to be more alarmed! With our family is Leslie Arends, a former Minority Whip in the U.S. House of Representatives, a Republican whom I knew well from my Illinois days.

Our 1985 Winter Commencement brought together two men quite unlikely to appear on the same stage; in fact, they usually were like oil and water to each other: Lane Kirkland, long-time president of the AFL-CIO and William F. Buckley, conservative author, commentator and founder of National Review – both natives of Camden, SC.

term as Secretary of State and Governor. From there he served for 30 years as one of Oregon's U.S. Senators and was a great friend of our own Senator Fritz Hollings. I met him when I was at the Lilly Endowment in the mid-1970s. We became fast friends, and he even nominated me to be president at Carolina in 1977. After he facilitated a $16 million grant to help with the construction of the Swearingen Engineering Center, I asked Hatfield to speak at our December 20, 1987 commencement. When his son, Vincent (nickname Visco), an undergraduate intern in my office, crossed the stage to receive his degree, he was wearing dark glasses and was being led by a guide dog – although Visco was not blind. The audience cheered. Visco's irreverence on such an occasion was an amusement to everyone. Except maybe his father!

Somewhere along the way, I dispensed with mortarboards and their tassels for dignitaries to be seated on the commencement stages. Some of these already had received honorary degrees or addressed the graduating class before that decision was reached. Others seemed relieved not to be bothered with a tassel swaying as they processed.

"Why has America succeeded for over two centuries in its democracy and preservation of freedom? In large part it is because of love and commitment. The greater the internal self-restraint born of love and commitment, the lesser the need for external controls such as governments impose upon their people. No super power or summit, no congressional legislation, and no preacher from the pulpit can mandate morality or control ego or greed." – *Mark Hatfield*

When Sen. Mark Hatfield was our Winter Commencement speaker at the end of our Ecumenical Year, we still were basking in the afterglow of the Pope's visit. His son Visco was in the graduating class.

Alex Haley, author of "Roots," exchanges points of view with Bill Cosby. Both spoke at the Spring 1986 Commencement.

Awaiting the processional for the Winter 1986 Commencement to begin are: Provost Frank Borkowski, left, the Rev. Dr. Billy Graham, USC Board Chairman Othniel Wienges and the Rev. Frank Harrington, pastor of Peachtree Presbyterian Church in Atlanta.

USC Coastal Carolina uproariously applauded the commencement appearance of Jim Brady, former Press Secretary to President Reagan, center, and his wife Sara. Carolyn and I were so proud of the inspiration the seriously wounded Brady gave those graduates.

Harold Krents, author of "To Race the Wind" and blind Harvard Law graduate, left; with Francois Michelin, Chairman and CEO of Michelin Tires; and Gian Carlo Menotti, the founder of the Spoleto Festival.

Gian Carlo Menotti, left, Markley Dennis, and Harold Krents, nationally acclaimed author.

Carolyn welcomes Alex Haley.

At my inauguration in December 1977, the speaker was Juanita Kreps, Secretary of Labor in the Carter Administration. She was seated on the platform next to S.C. Governor James B. Edwards.

Chris Vlahoplus, USC Vice President and Secretary of the University Board of Trustees, left, assists USC Board Chairman Othniel Wienges in hooding Greek Archbishop of the Western Hemisphere Iakovos with his regalia when he received an honorary degree from USC.

The last commencement ceremony over which I presided brought together South Carolina Governor Carroll Campbell, to my left, Kitty Carlisle Hart, Mike Mungo, President George Bush, First Lady Barbara Bush, Michael Eisner, Andrew Lloyd Webber, 1985 U.S. Teacher of the Year, and South Carolinian Terry Dozier.

Graduates will remember that a sitting president was their commencement speaker. This was the second time George H. W. Bush was on our campus during my administration; the first time he was Vice President.

U.S. President George H.W. Bush.

The First Lady of the United States, Barbara Bush.

Presidential observation: George was a regular guy and Barbara a great lady.

An honorary degree does not stack up very well against being President of the United States, yet Reagan accepted ours.

Reagan gets an armful of Gamecock souvenirs at a Horseshoe convocation. This was the first visit by a U.S. President since early in the 20th century.

U.S. President Ronald Reagan and U.S. Senator Strom Thurmond.

Reagan came to USC for the Horseshoe Honorary Doctorate presentation and attended a reception in honor of Senator Strom Thurmond later the same day in 1983. On the right is Governor Richard W. Riley.

USC awarded an honorary degree to Augusta Baker, the University's first Storyteller-in-Residence, in 1986.

When U.S. Senator Joe Biden came to Carolina, he was not yet Vice President of the United States.

Armand Hammer, CEO,
OCCIDENTAL PETROLEUM

"Thank you, Lord. That Lil' president fella hasn't cornered me for a big contribution (yet!) but, I suppose it's only a matter of time!"

Mr. Hammer was right: "Twas only a matter of time!"

This student explains why he was catching some last minute rays – so he wouldn't look so pale in his cap and gown.

Mister Rogers being welcomed by USC mascot, Cocky, to the latter's own "beautiful neighborhood" in Carolina country at the Spring Commencement in 1985. USC board member, William Bethea, left, and ex officio member and State Superintendent of Education Charles Williams, right, register their approval.

Bricks and Mortar

Surfacing early among my assessments of faculty and student contentment was legitimate grousing about the condition of buildings, the lack of adequate lab equipment, faculty compensation and other observations. I took these seriously and began immediately to remedy those realities. Nonetheless, in gauging how USC stacked up, I took a great deal more into account than merely bricks and mortar. Brain, the most essential factor in the collegiate equation, was intrinsic, therein hard to measure, although it was tested and ranked frequently. Brawn – or, Athletics, had its own scoreboards. Although I heard a litany of complaints about Athletics, usually on Monday mornings, never did I hear a single complaint that USC placed too much emphasis on Athletics.

The first official phone call I made as President-elect of the University was to Sol Blatt, already in his early eighties. The Speaker Emeritus of the South Carolina House of Representatives had served as Speaker longer than any other leader in a democratically-elected parliament in the world – over 50 years. He loved the House and he loved USC where he had been a cheerleader in the early 20th century. He never stopped being its cheerleader. He worked all his professional life to converge the interest of his two greatest institutional loves, the House and Carolina. The USC Board of Trustees and even Republican Governor Jim Edwards advised me to speak first to the former, but still formidable, Democratic Speaker of the House. He impressed me immediately by being warm and friendly, and invited me and my family to Barnwell to a seafood dinner. The enduring friendship we began that day was strong enough to survive one or two skirmishes.

One involved my naming a vice president for Athletics, an attempt to reduce the insatiable appetite for control of football coach Jim Carlen. The concept may not have been a good one, but I had made my move. Carlen exploded. Speaker Blatt called me shortly before noon one day in that spring of 1978. His precise message was to back down, cancel

Giving assurance and probably some stability to the University's School of Medicine was one of my first initiatives, so I was especially pleased to speak at one of their first commencements. A major contention was the size of each freshman class in the School of Medicine. Opponents of USC's School of Medicine were determined to keep the entering class small, therefore restricting its overall growth. Thankfully, those folks have not prevailed. USC's med school is now competitive with the best.

the VP slot and acknowledge my error. He said I would look the "bigger" man for doing so. I told him I did not agree and would not change the course. He said, "Mr. President, I am not used to being spoken to like that." I replied, "Well, Mr. Speaker, I'm not either." His response was a click, and he was gone.

Friends in his office that noon reported to me later that the hat he had donned for lunch was practically bobbing atop his head he was so angry. In about 20 minutes, while I was seriously considering cleaning out my desk, Speaker Blatt called me back. He said, "Dr. Holderman, I am sorry I spoke to you like that. I respect you for standing up for what you believe, even though I do not agree. You do not have to worry about my friendship; it is yours. I trust you will accept it." I said, "Mr. Speaker, I appreciate your call and even more importantly, your friendship, and I shall always treasure it." I always did. We were fast friends from then on. I stopped cleaning out my desk.

John Swearingen

The John E. Swearingen Engineering Center

By the mid-1980's, it became apparent to me that South Carolina's future economy was going to require a larger number of graduates in the engineering sciences. A 30-year old building had fallen into disrepair and lacked the technology that would be required for our graduates to enter their chosen fields with competitive edges.

Luckily, a South Carolina native of Columbia and Carolina graduate, John Swearingen, had enjoyed great success in the oil business. He was the retired Chairman and CEO of Standard Oil of Indiana (briefly AMOCO and now BP, British Petroleum) and rescuer of Chicago's

Cocky, Carolina's alter ego, characterizes the institution's brawn, but encourages the brain as well.

John Swearingen, shovel in hand, breaks ground for the new engineering center, which bears his name. To my right is USC Trustee Chairman Othniel Wienges. Cocky is unmistakable.

Continental Illinois Bank. During a trip to Chicago to witness the installation of Archbishop Joseph Bernardin, another Columbia native and great friend, I went to see John. I asked for his support in building a new engineering school to be named for him. John was initially reluctant, but his wife, Bonnie, saw the vision and opportunity.

By the time I left John's office, he and Bonnie had given me the names, on the back of an envelope, of several dozen oil magnates around the country they thought might honor John in this way and help build the new center. With $16 million dollars' assistance in federal funds sponsored by U.S. Senator Mark Hatfield from Oregon, Chairman of the Senate Finance Committee, we built an engineering school that added scores of state-of-the-art labs, and more than 100,000 additional square feet of classroom and office space. An attractive feature of the engineering complex is an atrium in the center, designed for small concerts and receptions.

The center offers research in computer technology, machine intelligence, and other new fields, as well as traditional engineering fields. Getting our students into that facility really put USC on the map in the emerging fields; was then, and still is, a great accomplishment of which I remain justifiably proud. Sixteen million dollars from a federal grant, combined with approximately fifteen million dollars in private contributions, made it all possible. In addition, the exceptional gift of an SCE&G building across the street greatly enhanced the facility and the site.

On the very morning of the scheduled groundbreaking for the John E. Swearingen Engineering Center with properly accompanying ceremonies, I learned the hard fact that the land upon which the ceremony and subsequent construction were to occur was not (quite) yet the deeded property of the University of South Carolina! Upon hearing that disturbing news, I immediately contacted former governor Robert McNair, often our quite remarkable savior in such situations. When he was told of our dilemma, he quickly contacted the owner of the property, Norfolk and Southern Railway, where he had strong connections. The governor delivered "big time" for his alma mater that day as he arranged for the property's immediate purchase.

Bonnie Swearingen, left, and her husband John Swearingen, right, admire a watercolor painting of the Horseshoe gates by Guy Lipscomb, a loyal alumnus, enterprising industrialist, generous benefactor and award-winning artist.

The Ira and Nancy Koger Center for the Arts

The change of family ownership at *The State* newspaper to Knight-Ridder, Inc. gave us hope some of that transitional money would help complete the arts center. After all, it had been Mayor Kirk Finlay, husband of the newspaper's largest stakeholder, who had come to me early one Sunday morning, along with my very special friend, distinguished civic leader, Stan Smith, to lay out the concept. They brought me a proposal for the land on which the center could be sited.

In hopes of strengthening the possibility of attracting the necessary funds locally, I went to Jacksonville, Florida, to have a face-to-face conversation with Ira Koger regarding the naming of the center. After all, his generous financial commitment had been essential and foundational to the start-up of the undertaking. I asked him if it would be alright with him if the auditorium were named Gonzales Hall, a civic nod to the founders of *The State* newspaper. He agreed.

Opening night was approaching fast, and while Mayor Patton Adams was out of the country, one of the City of Columbia's inspectors showed up and told us we would not be able to open, that rails in the balconies were not high enough to meet code. With Mayor Adams unavailable to override the inspector's edict, I ignored the pink slip. To myself I said, "Like hell we won't open!" We opened.

In my inaugural remarks that rainy evening, I said: "We have been waiting on this building for more than two decades. Some people think we should have waited two more weeks."

What a thrill it was for us to have the London Philharmonic Orchestra perform for the opening concert! The orchestra always begins its performances with "God Save the Queen." What many of us heard was our familiar "My Country 'Tis of Thee," and figured the world renowned orchestra was paying tribute to its host country because the music is exactly the same.

Ira Koger had presented himself to me as an expert on music, so I chalked it up to his enthusiasm and pride that he was the only one in the audience to applaud during Mahler's Tenth, a composition which has no separate movements.

Among the priorities I recognized upon my arrival at USC in the summer of 1977 were the conspicuous needs for a state-of-the-art performing arts center, a new engineering

I admit it: the Koger Center was my baby. It was also Chris Vlahoplus and Tommy Stepp's baby. To finally see it lit up in all its splendor was an emotional moment of accomplishment for all the University.

Ira Koger, for whom the Koger Center is named.

Finally, after many frustrating delays, we broke ground for the Koger Center. Mayor Kirkman Finlay, second from left, was instrumental in the undertaking.

school, a medical school and land for overall expansion. We had academic standards and money to raise, but the campus in Columbia, and several of the system campuses, cried out for attention. The General Assembly's earlier interest in long-term financing of education facilities was becoming undependable and we needed public and private sources of funds for both architectural planning and construction. Kicking the can down the road was not a strategy I could embrace.

But like many efforts to bring any kind of change, I found myself having to fight for every dollar and defend against those who saw these improvements as reflections of my expansive self. Not so! But that didn't stop even my friend, Robert Ariail, cartoonist at *The State* newspaper, from lampooning my Sandcastles. Those sandcastles helped improve the quality of education and life on our Columbia campus, and they are still here, not yet washed away by a projected tsunami.

Carolyn with Ira and Nancy Koger. The reception was in their honor.

The Holdermans and the Kogers became good friends.

Among the myriad additions to the University during my tenure, one of which I continue to be proud is the film archives from Movietone News. Lowell Thomas, seen on screen, was instrumental in making Carolina a prime contender for the footage. Here, faculty and administrators are introduced to what we have acquired.

Movietone News

Early in 1980, we signed the agreement with Twentieth Century Fox for USC to become the repository of approximately one hundred million feet of newsreel film.

To seal the transaction, Twentieth Century Fox honored us at a reception at the Madison Hotel in Washingtion, D.C. where samples of the news clips were shown. Seated in the audience were ambassadors from both Germany and Japan. What flashed up on the screen in that darkened room filled with dignitaries and business tycoons were clips from WWII in which the U.S. was defeating Germany and Japan. Those two ambassadors sat through it bravely, said not a word, and made quick exits as soon as the screening was over.

Even now when I see a few frames of archival footage used in a film, a commercial, a presentation, I think about the great coup it was for USC to become the repository of this priceless documentation of our history.

I often recall a moment that made the import of all that footage very real for me. We were in L.A. to play Southern California (yes, you remember correctly: we lost), but on that football trip, we (the Board of Trustees, University

George Rogers upon the retirement of his number 38 jersey. George was being swarmed by well-wishers who wanted his autograph. He turned to me and said, "Dr. Holderman, I want YOUR autograph." I quickly asked him, "Where?" He said, "On my diploma!"

Here I am between brawn and brain. George Rogers, left, raised the University's visibility nationally. He also was successful off the playing field; he helped secure for the University the continuation of our General Studies associate degree program by visiting the State House where he explained to lawmakers how important the program was for first generation college students. George, who just a month earlier had won the Heisman Trophy, completed his degree in the College of General Studies. At right is Rhodes Scholar Daniel Dreisbach, USC Spartanburg 1981, of whom we were also very very proud. Universities don't receive such recognition that often and seldom at the same time.

This quilt is made from the academic hoods that I received during my career in higher education.

Officers, and their families) were guests at the FOX movie studios on the lot where M.A.S.H. was filmed. I was invited to sit at the desk of Col. Sherman Potter, commanding officer in the long-running and hugely popular M.A.S.H. series. The Colonel, Radar and Hawkeye had long since left the set, but their presence certainly was felt. The evening was meant to celebrate the Movietone gift: the historic news footage we had received from 20th Century FOX.

What a fine day it was when I picked up *The State* and read, quite unexpectedly, that Clemson President Bill Atchley had written the editor his congratulations to me and the University on the acquisition of the Movietone News archives.

From Bill's letter: *"I congratulate Dr. Holderman and his associates on such a significant achievement and for helping raise the standards of private support in higher education in South Carolina."*

So, Bill clearly recognized the import of this transaction! He also noted that the national spotlight the Movietone News collection will focus upon this state could add a significant boost to efforts by Clemson, USC and other schools to augment private giving.

To whom much is given, much is expected. Our eldest daughter Betsy, an accomplished and giving young woman, received the Algernon Sydney Sullivan Award. Since 1890, this recognition has been made at more than 60 colleges and universities in the American South to individuals whose "nobility of character and service to others set them apart as examples to others." How proud of her I was – and am!

The Ecumenical Year

"The Breath of God," the sermon given in our historic Rutledge Chapel the morning of the Pope's visit, simplified what we had sought so fully over preceding months. In explaining his sermon's theme, the Rev. Don Jones, Chairman of the University's Religion Department, suggested that God's spirit was at work in the gatherings in Columbia that unforgettable day.

Two years of planning preceded Pope John Paul II's visit to Columbia. I knew that every second of that momentous day, the University of South Carolina, our city and state would be on the world stage, and that every moment would be judged for its success or failure.

To frame the visit with an appropriate theme that melded with the Pope's own mission – building unity and dialogue among the world's Christian denominations, we conceived a plan to organize and observe a Year of Ecumenism throughout our System and throughout South Carolina.

Accepting our invitations were spritual leaders whose presence and words helped lay the foundation within the myriad denominations in anticipation of the arrival of world religious leaders who would meet privately with the Pope on this subject on the second floor of the President's House after greeting students, faculty and guests on the Horseshoe.

Participants described the afternoon meeting, which brought together the Pope and 23 other religious leaders, as undoubtedly the most important ecumenical event in American religious history. That morning, the leaders had worshipped together at the historic Rutledge Chapel as Rev. Dr. Don Jones, a United Methodist minister and then-chairman of USC's Religious Studies department, described the spiritual climate enveloping the gathering as "The Breath of God."

When I first saw the Popemobile reach the northern entry into the Horseshoe, followed by the security escort, my heart leapt at the same time as the hearts of thousands who began assembling there as early at 7:30 that morning. Could this be the most important thing I would ever do in my time on earth: to facilitate the convening of an unprecedented and historic meeting of the world's religious leadership, here in the Deep South – in this Carolina?

In my welcome I called the Pope's visit the high point of the University of South Carolina's

On the second floor of the President's House, ecumenical history was made when Pope John Paul II met with leaders representing Christian denominations throughout the United States. The cloistered meeting was open only to these selected faith leaders; however, a photographer caught a glimpse of the gathering through the window.

Robert Ariail's cartoon of the four holy men portrayed, left to right: Archbishop Robert Runcie, Archbishop Iakovos, Pope John Paul II, and the Rev. Dr. Billy Graham.

FOR JIM ~
personal regards
12.6.86.
12/21/86

Ecumenical Year of Observance, and referred to those leaders with whom he would meet shortly on the second floor of the President's House. He concluded his remarks to the students by saying:

"It is wonderful to be young!
It is wonderful to be young and a student at the University!
It is wonderful to be young and a student at the University of South Carolina!"
– Pope John Paul II

That quotation is captured on a bronze plaque in front of the President's house on the Horseshoe.

When it was nearly time to leave for Williams Brice Stadium, I knocked, then entered the room where the Pope had been resting. He asked me how long the upcoming interdenominational service might last. I told him I thought it might run three to four hours, and he thanked me and said he thought he'd use the adjoining restroom while he could.

Actor Michael Keaton was among the recognizable personalities who added grace and talent to the service at Williams-Brice Stadium that hot September afternoon.

So USC has a commode used by the Pope, as well as many other more notable memories and images from that remarkable day: September 11, 1987.

My friend Robert Ariail, cartoonist for *The State* newspaper, had drawn a four-subject portrait of the quartet of leaders representing religious denominations coming to visit USC: Greek Archbishop Iakovos of North and South America, Anglican Archbishop of Canterbury Robert Runcie, Christian evangelist Rev. Dr. Billy Graham, and Pope John Paul II of the Roman Catholic Church. The first three had kindly autographed their images during their visits.

On the day we were hosting the Holy Father on the USC campus, I had the cartoon placed on an easel in the guest room on the second floor of the President's House (named the Kennedy Room because the future American President, then a U.S. Senator from Massachusetts, had stayed there during his commencement visit in 1957.) With the cartoon was a pen attached by a string. I hoped that the Holy Father might sign it as well. I overheard his advisors suggesting that he not do so. However, he did. His signature is in Latin: Joannes Paulus II.

Recently, President Harris Pastides had the cartoon copied and beautifully framed for me. It is one of my most prized possessions. The original is in USC's McKissick Museum's collection.

The Rev. Dr. Billy Graham, right, for whom a Columbia stop was on his summer 1986 crusade schedule, agreed to speak to our graduating class at Winter Commencement, a presence which helped launch and set the tone for our Year of Ecumenism.

Archbishop Iakovos, center, is seated next to Columbia Mayor Patton Adams during a luncheon following his receipt of an honorary degree from Carolina.

Greek Archbishop Iakovos signs the Robert Ariail cartoon depicting the four holy men who were linchpins in the unprecedented Ecumenical Year.

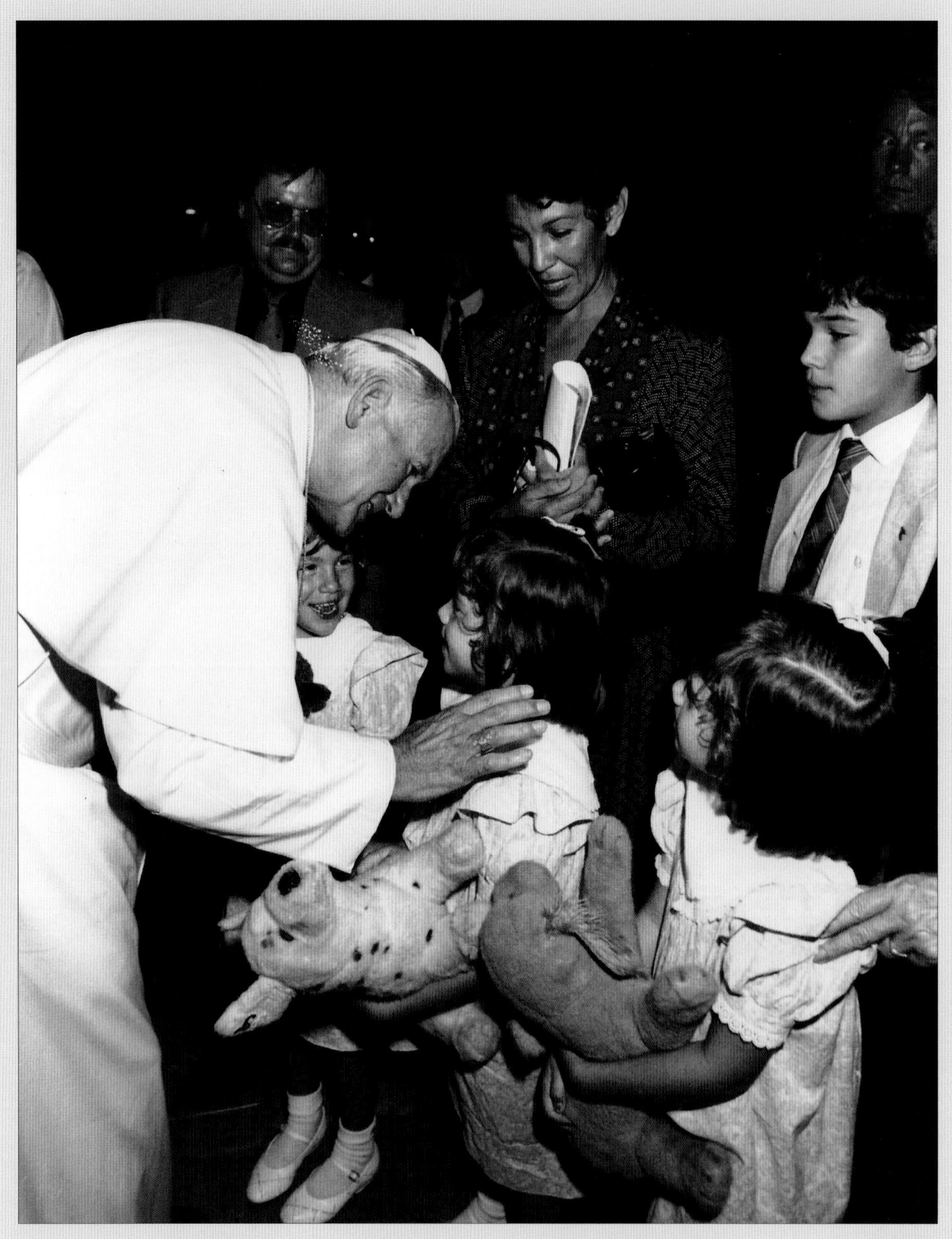

At St. Peter's Catholic Church, the first stop on the Pope's itinerary, the Holy Father blesses the children – and their "pets."

The Papal Visit

The morning of September 11th, 1987, began on a wet, dark Friday dawn. As I awakened, I felt a strange mixture of conflicting expectations. I knew that day would shape up to be the most moving experience of my personal and professional life or a disaster of immeasurable embarrassment.

To be sure, whatever happened would put the University of South Carolina, the City of Columbia, and the State of South Carolina in the annals of our history and on the world stage, and every moment of the day would be measured for its success or failure.

I blinked several times, breathed deeply and rose to face a day that could never be equaled again in my life. A farm boy from Morris, Illinois – deep in the corn country of rural mid-West America – was to host none other than the most important leader on the planet and two dozen religious leaders from around the world to close out an ambitious year of ecumenism that would be crowned by the most unlikely visit of Pope John Paul II to the heart of the South.

Thanks to the initial invitation of the Bishop of the Catholic Diocese of Charleston, the Most Reverend Ernest Unterkoefler, who had been chairing a National Council of Catholic Bishops' committee on ecumenism, and the critical intercession of Joseph Cardinal Bernardin, Archbishop of Chicago, native of Columbia and Chairman of USC's National Advisory Council, the Holy Father had agreed to make a stop in Columbia on his nine city visit to the United States.

His Holiness had been elected Pope nine years earlier on October 16th, 1978, and was the first non-Italian to head the Roman Catholic Church since Dutchman Adrian VI, who died in 1523.

By the time the morning of September 11th, 1987 arrived, every contingency had been anticipated. The night before, Bishop William Beckham of the Upper Diocese of the Episcopal Church of South Carolina and a good friend throughout these proceedings, served as a host of a private dinner for the assembling World Religious Leadership on the seventeenth floor of USC's Capstone building.

The next morning all eyes and ears turned to news at the Columbia Airport. The Pope's plane had departed from its first American city, Miami, some twenty minutes late, but we all were relieved to learn that two advance planes carrying the Vatican press corps and staff had landed safely at 3:15 p.m. and 3:20 p.m., followed in ten minutes by the Pontiff's own Shepard I, right on time.

After adjusting the ramp, the door of Shepard I, decorated by the papal coat of arms, opened. Several Roman Catholic dignitaries descended, followed by Pope John Paul II dressed in white and clinging to his Zucchepto (white cap) to keep it from blowing off his head amidst the airport winds.

An official delegation of South Carolina Roman Catholic clergy and state political leadership gathered at the bottom of the ramp to welcome His Holiness. He was greeted by Governor Carroll Campbell and his wife, Iris; U.S. Senator Strom Thurmond; U.S. Senator Fritz Hollings, and his Catholic wife, Peatsy, who kissed the Pope's ring, a Catholic tradition; Columbia Mayor Patton Adams; Sr. M. Anne Francis Campbell, General Superior of the Sisters of Charity of Our Lady of Mercy of Charleston; and Father Christine Carr, Abbott of Mepkin Abbey.

Soon, John Paul II and his entourage was making its way to Columbia, and he was able to read the first of 190 banners and 5 billboards in yellow, white, and purple proclaiming, "Witamy Papieza" (Polish: Welcome, Holy Father).

The Pope's route into the city was kept a secret for security purposes and crowd control, both of which were overblown by sensationalism of news forecasting and the overzealousness of local officials, which in my opinion, depressed the turnout of the public at the several viewing opportunities provided them. No good deed goes unpunished.

Now it was the Catholic community's turn to greet their leader in Saint Peter's Catholic Church on Assembly Street. It was certainly appropriate for the Holy Father to begin his visit to Columbia at the home church of his dear friend, Columbia native, Joseph Cardinal Bernardin, Archbishop of Chicago.

The Pope's moving visit to St. Peter's, which had begun with a choir singing the third verse of "Stainless the Maiden" in Polish, ended with the Pope's praise for South Carolina Catholics' history of ecumenism. The Holy Father thanked the congregation for its "famous hospitality."

After 44 minutes at St Peter's, Pope John Paul II headed for the USC Horseshoe in his Popemobile.

As the Pope entered the Horseshoe the crowd spontaneously took up the chant: "John Paul II, we love you." And he responded, "John Paul II loves you, too!"

Many who had been displaced from the dorm rooms and offices on the Horseshoe for security reasons had somehow produced hundreds of blue t-shirts reading "I Was Moved By The Pope."

The crowd chased the Popemobile as it made its majestic drive around the Horseshoe to stop in front of the platform erected in front of the President's House. Joined then by my wife Carolyn and members of the University's Trustees, I looked into the warm eyes of the Holy Father. His smile reflected his appreciation of even more Southern hospitality.

In my welcoming remarks, I called the Pope's visit "the high point of the University of South Carolina's Ecumenical Year of Observance." I praised the Pope for doing more for "ecclesiastical bridge-building in your pontificate than in hundreds of years." Referring to our historic Horseshoe, I said: "You bring it peace, Holy Father, for you are the symbol of peace."

The Pope concluded his warm remarks to the crowd with an impromptu response to the enthusiasm he absorbed from the students who had refreshed and impressed him.

Before His Holiness left the podium to meet with the assembled religious leaders on the second floor of the President's House, Student Body President Michael Hogue presented him with a Polish dulcimer, in violation of all instructions not to present gifts of any kind. Unhesitatingly, the Pope graciously accepted the dulcimer and promised the large, admiring crowd that he would play it.

Then the Pope went to work in an 80-minute private dialogue with the 26 leaders seated in the second floor foyer of the President's House. Just after 6:30 p.m., the Pope emerged from the house and went to the podium to adress the crowd of students that had dwindled to about 3,000.

"South Carolina, do you pray? If you do, pray for me."

– Pope John Paul II

Then he left the USC campus for an ecumenical service at Williams Brice Stadium in the company of the religious leaders, an assembly of special guests, and an audience of 60,000 people.

I found His Holiness both serene and congenial. I had heard that when he deplaned his frequent flights he was queried about why he kissed the ground. He was known to reply: "If you flew Alitalia as often as I do, you'd kiss the ground too!"

All the World's a Stage

Carolina's curtain goes up for actors, entertainers and sports figures

For the University of South Carolina to mirror even a little of the glitter that already had befallen stars of stage and screen could only add to our luster. Luminaries who came to visit, and often to teach, had perfected their craft in various schools of hard knocks. The examples they set and the lessons they imparted to students were invaluable.

In the South perhaps it is possible for a man to have a dowry, as did women in earlier centuries. If so, mine was the friendship of Helen Hayes, "First Lady of The American Theater" and one of the most wonderful and absorbing people I ever had the privilege to know. Her audacity was breathtaking, and there was no end to her kindnesses and gestures of support. She co-chaired USC's 1983-84 Summit Fund Campaign and established several scholarships in her name in the Department of Theater and Dance.

When I was in her company, her graciousness made me so comfortable that I accomplished the feat of both remembering and forgetting who I was with – at the same time. We had been acquainted for a while, initially, in regard to an attempt to build the Helen Hayes MacArthur Center for the Arts adjacent to the University of Illinois at Chicago Circle. I was looking forward to meeting her for lunch in New York City at the Edwardian Room at the Plaza Hotel. By then I had known her long enough for her to ask that I call her "Helen" – which, of course, I loved. I had called the restaurant weeks in advance, and several times, to assure we would be seated at the very best table.

As we were into the elegant salad course, a distinguished chap approached the table. She put her hand in his and their conversation flowed as naturally as the talk of old friends is expected to. She remarked with no hesitation to the other fellow, "I know you two know each other well." To which he nodded agreeably. When he walked away, Helen glowed. "Richard's music is what I love best, don't you?" The encroaching gentleman had been Richard Rodgers. I said, "This has been some enchanted evening!"

In 1987, Pope John Paul II, left, takes the hand of Helen Hayes who was on the program for the Ecumenical Service at Williams Brice Stadium. Helen later told me she wore white so she might be mistaken as the Pope's wife!

Through Helen, I found myself on a first-name basis with countless luminaries – sometimes in person, more often in conversations with her. Larry was Laurence Olivier, Mary was Martin, John was Barrymore, Scott was Fitzgerald and Jimmy, with whom she did "Harvey," was Jimmy Stewart – whom I met when he came to USC to make a commencement address. When he was on campus, thanks to Helen, he was besieged following commencement by well wishers seeking his autograph. I asked, "Jimmy, do you want me to free you from these folks?" He said politely but firmly, "Heavens no, they have been paying my salary for decades! If they want my autograph, that is the least I can do!"

But it was when she spoke to God that I found Helen's audacity the most exhilarating. I saw her turn heavenward early in an out-of-doors USC-Spartanburg Commencement in 1978, amidst very dark clouds and thundering rumble. She exclaimed in remarks conspicuously addressed to the Almighty: "Jehovah, I am doing the best I can; behave yourself." He did. The storm held off until the end of the ceremonies.

Speaking of audacity: long before that manifestation of her familiarity and obvious status with the Almighty, I had seen Helen Hayes stare down protesters at a University of Illinois-Chicago Circle Commencement. We had been warned that some of the graduating class felt Miss Hayes' honorary degree was irrelevant. She had been hooded and moved to the rostrum when some protesters began to stand. She thanked the audience "from the bottom of my heart for the honor you have seen fit to bestow upon me today – and also from the bottom of that most grateful heart, I am constrained to say: 'It's about time!' You see, my romance with the City of Chicago began about fifty years ago and, though I have been honored and recognized in other cities, always there was an ache in my heart that my true love had not seen fit to notice me." She had held them at bay. They quieted and sat back down.

When I left USC under duress, Helen was invited to nominate candidates to replace me. She answered the letter Mark Buyck sent on July 5, 1990:

"As I am familiar with the situation and the reason for Jim's resignation of the presidency, it seems to me that any suggestion that I could make would be dangerous. My thinking is so different from that of the Board of Trustees at the University and the press of Columbia, South Carolina, that I would hesitate to recommend anyone other than someone that I admire and respect, wholeheartedly, as I do Jim Holderman. From now on I have no further connections with the University."

The tiny but powerful woman who signed that letter had quite a way with words.

Our time to have Jimmy Stewart with us for May Commencement 1988 happened to fall close to his birthday, so Carolyn arranged for him to be presented with a birthday cake.

Gloria and Jimmy Stewart, Carolyn and I were at the dinner the night before commencement in 1988.

I continue to credit Helen as having played a leading role in putting the University of South Carolina on the world stage – through the connections she elicited and through her inspiration. She was an accomplished Shakespearean actress and certainly gave her blessing to the University's partnership with the Folger Shakespearean Library in Washington, D.C. When *The New York Times* reported on the agreement, it emphasized acting apprenticeships and internships at the Folger for university students, and an adjunct professorship for a theater professional at the university's Columbia campus.

Ed Hennessy, center, chairman and CEO of Allied Signal, renews his acquaintance with Helen Hayes, his co-chair of the Summit Fund from 1979-1980.

Jimmy Stewart sat at the baby grand piano at the President's House on the evening before he was to be our commencement speaker and played barroom tunes from his earliest days in show business. For those days, the lyrics were "racy" – not for this day, though – and some of the tunes were Jimmy's own. Perhaps he had been playing himself all those years.

Fred Rogers was asked to speak at commencement in 1985, and the law students protested the invitation. I called the vocal leadership to my office and heard them out. They said Fred Rogers was not sophisticated enough for their graduation. I told them I had met him when I was at the Lilly Endowment just before I came to Carolina and had given him a grant for his Children's Television Workshop program. Then I told them that Fred had been a storied Navy SEAL, alleged to have killed men with his bare hands, and that the numerous tattoos up and down both arms were covered by his mother's hand-knitted sweaters for his appearances on television. He became an ordained Presbyterian minister after the war. Then I asked the law students if they knew who had delivered the commencement address

Fred Rogers delighted the children he met while he was with us for a commencement exercise in 1985 – and brought out the children in us all.

Fred Rogers, Mister Rogers to America, received the honorary degree in 1985.

at Harvard the year before. They didn't. I said truthfully: "Kermit, the frog." Jim Henson's daughter was graduating that year from Harvard and Kermit spoke. That ended the objection to Mister Rogers. In fact, he sang to our graduates, "I love you,' and they sang back, "We love you!" It was a wonderful day in our neighborhood.

Michael Eisner, Disney CEO, arrived to be our May 1990 commencement speaker, only one week after both *The State* newspaper and *The Charlotte Observer* had eviscerated me for what their reporters and editors considered lavish spending. Eisner had been in the same college fraternity I was in, but at a different time. From the podium he could have made me look good. Instead, he cracked: "So that explains why Jim had to have the presidential suite in our fraternity house at Denison University." Just what I needed!

The critical news was in response to our staying and dining at the Pierre Hotel in New York when we went to meet with a well-known and major prospective donor. I explained to the Board of Trustees that the potential donor did not want to meet in a very public place, so we didn't. The prospect seemed ready to help us raise a large amount of money for the foundation and university. It seemed to me, whatever accommodation we needed to make in order to meet with him on his terms, was a reasonable investment. His interest in the University left with me, unfortunately.

Robby Benson and his wife Karla became great assets to Carolina through the cultivation of our personal relationship, a strategy that worked to benefit the university throughout my tenure.

Carolina gave Robby an Honorary Degree in the 1980s, and he and Karla fell in love with Columbia and moved here to take positions as Artists in Residence in our Masters in Fine Arts program. He had starred in *Ice Castles, Ode to Billy Joe* and *One on One*, and performed with Paul Newman, Jack Lemmon, Burt Reynolds, Ossie Davis, George Burns and many others.

In his recent memoir, *I'm Not Dead ... Yet!*, he describes his experiences at Carolina generously and writes especially kind words about me, saying I was a " very persuasive President ... and a great fundraiser and a forward-thinker ... Dr. Holderman turned the University from a party school in 1977 to the number one international business graduate school in the nation."

While on campus, Robby rewrote his film "Modern Love" and set it in South Carolina, using Carolina students and giving them a chance to learn the trade and earn money working on a feature film.

Robby has survived four open-heart surgeries for a congenital heart defect and is now on the faculty of Indiana University in Bloomington, Indiana, and is still making films. Several of his surgeries have resulted in the implantation of swine parts into his system. In fact, if you ask him politely about that, he is likely to "oink" for you. He did that for me a number of times.

President George H.W. Bush and Barbara Bush were our guests May 12, 1990 at com-

Michael Eisner, right, Disney's CEO, came for the May 1990 commencement, the last over which I presided.

Bill Cosby was not bored; he was thinking up what he could do to bring the house down, and he did. He invited parents to be greeted, along with their graduating sons and daughters. He made sure I had to shake hundreds more hands that day than I had anticipated. My hand was in a cast, so I remember it well.

mencement on the Columbia campus along with Michael Eisner of Disney, and British composer Andrew Lloyd Webber. Also with us that day was the actress Kitty Carlisle Hart, widow of the late American composer Moss Hart. At a dinner in honor of our overnight guests, Carolyn sat between Kitty Carlisle Hart and Andrew Lloyd Webber. That year, Webber had four musicals playing on Broadway: *Cats, Starlight Express, Phantom of the Opera* and *Aspects of Love.* The productions were all big hits, and several played on Broadway for years. During the dinner Carolyn turned to Kitty and asked her which musicals then on Broadway were her favorite. Kitty said loudly and without hesitation: "None of them." She preferred the music of her husband, Moss Hart, and Richard Rodgers, to that of her dinner partner Webber. He said nothing, thankfully, and Carolyn escaped without embarrassment. Those dinners were fun but, with so many egos in the room, they had their moments.

The next day, as we awaited graduation ceremonies and the presentation of a musical tribute that Robby Benson and Karla DeVito had created in honor of Lloyd Webber's visit, I received an urgent call from Tommy Stepp. According to Tommy, the Lloyd Webber folks were upset because they believed Robby and Karla did not get the copyright permissions they needed to use Andrew's works, and he was threatening to go home right then! Webber was to receive an honorary degree at graduation. I managed to get through to him on the phone in his suite at the Marriott and persuaded him to meet me for coffee in the Koger Center to discuss what could be done about the possible debacle. Finally, he agreed to stay for graduation, but on the condition that he keep his appointment with his pilot to take off from Columbia Airport by his self-imposed deadline, 3 p.m. The musical tribute to him was to begin early that afternoon. I knew it would go long. The only thing that could have made that day worse would have been for him to get up and leave in the middle of a tribute created just for him. I sweated out the entire performance. He didn't flinch, did not get up to leave. He missed his 3 p.m. departure time and, immediately after the last encore, asked to be taken backstage to congratulate Robby and Karla. Backstage Eisner asked me what the show's cost was. I replied: about $100k. He said that for him to put on such a show would have run over $1,000,000! I then suggested that he share that info with local media.

Shortly before Danny Kaye joined us in Columbia, he learned he was to receive the French Medal of Honor a few months later. He received an honorary degree from the University of South Carolina in 1985.

Danny Kaye, known for his films in which music was a key element, led Carolina Alive.

Gale Sayers visited us for a ballgame weekend in 1980 after a knee injury cut short his NFL career. To pay tribute to him at the game, the University band played the theme from *Brian's Song*, the 1971 movie about Gale's former NFL roommate, Brian Piccolo. His presence tipped off rumors that I was looking at him as a possible Athletic Director. (Which I was!) Instead, Gale joined our administration to help recruit minority students. He was very successful. Gale helped raise the minority enrollment to 15%, the highest in the nation for similar institutions.

Soon after the wildly-anticipated arrival of Rudolph Nureyev for a performance that had to be held at the Coliseum, we were encouraged to call him Rudy – which we did. When we contracted with ballet's international superstar to come to Carolina, we knew the Koger Center would be nowhere near finished. That meant there was also no adequate dressing room for the celebrated Soviet-born dancer who had defected in 1961. The best we could come up with was a trailer; at least he would have the privacy of his own changing space, we thought. Following his spectacular performance accompanied by the USC Symphony, audience members leaving from the North exits were treated to an unexpected encore. Rudy was changing in the trailer, doors wide open. His hands were free even of a towel to obscure his famous frame. Au naturale, he waved at audience members returning to their cars.

We had hitched our wagon to a number of stars, and when they visited, they brought their luminosity with them.

One morning, just before the Carolina-Clemson game, a commotion out on the Horseshoe got my attention. When I went outside to look, I saw somebody doing wheelies on a tractor. How the driver had gotten it through the gates struck me as very enterprising. The young fellow at the wheel, I soon found out, was indeed not only a student but a cheerleader – obviously afflicted by pre-game fever. Alex

Gale Sayers visited the campus with his wife, Ardie, and assisted System VP for Community Affairs Jake Jennings in recruiting minority students for all nine campuses.

English actor Robert Morley, left, here to give the commencement address and receive an honorary degree in 1984, greets Trustee Lily Roland Hall in the European manner. Also pictured is Lily's husband, Dean Hall.

Jack Wellman, left, of Wellman Industries, gives some thought to what actor Robert Morley is telling him – and to the actor's bountiful pocket square.

Daniels figured, when he got caught, that he would get suspended from school. Something about his competitive spirit caught my attention, though; I got to know him and ultimately gave him a position as an intern in my office. In time I introduced him to Helen Hayes who became his "adopted grandma;" he now has a career in Hollywood, rising from a highly sought stuntman to director.

Alex Daniels is a USC grad who has literally turned Hollywood on its heels. Alex is now 59 years old, a motion picture stunt coordinator and 2nd unit director, vice president of the Stuntmen's Association of Motion Pictures and president of his own film company, Frog Prince Productions.

I first noticed this super energetic student when he borrowed his grandfather's tractor and drove it 25 miles to the Horseshoe just before a USC-Clemson game as a prank. USC Police immediately arrested him, but I was able to intervene as I saw this stunt unfold from the window in the President's House.

Alex was a cheerleader and performer in Campus Theater and musical groups on campus and around the Columbia community, Alex Daniels was everywhere! I once asked him if he ever bothered to go to class.

Rudolf Nureyev tours the Koger site with the project director and USC Vice President Tommy Stepp.

I invited him to be an intern in the President's Office largely to keep him out of trouble. That rarely succeeded. However, Alex was, in fact, a great student, a member of Omicron Delta Kappa leadership fraternity and Mortar Board.

"Jim Holderman is largely responsible for sending me out into a bigger world which has led to an interesting and blessed life," he recently wrote. "Through him, Helen Hayes became my 'adopted grandma' and a big influence on my life and career. Father William Wasson also became an enormous figure in my life and I am still involved with his Nuestra Pequenos Hermanos orphanages in Mexico, having recently served seven years on his board, which operates orphanages now in nine countries. Through Jim Holderman and his influence I learned that no world is too big."

I appreciate Alex's attributing his amazing life in the film business to his time at Carolina and am awfully glad he has survived the terrifying stunts he has performed in countless films.

Alex Daniels, JBH, Nancy Thurmond, Helen Hayes, Father William Wasson and George Curry

Pearl Bailey, right, lit up every room she entered, especially the Carolina Coliseum when she received an honorary degree and spoke at graduation.

Composer and conductor John Williams warms up the orchestra for a concert. The Boston Pops conductor brought the Pops here for concert during my tenure. He received an honorary degree early in my years at Carolina.

Helen Hayes, left, receives a bouquet of red roses from Glenn German, USC Student Body President. Later Glenn became a prominent screenwriter in Hollywood.

Helen Hayes, center, was interesting because she was interested – and so well informed on nearly every topic. Across from Helen, in foreground, is British Ambassador to the U.S., Sir Oliver Wright, husband of Lady Mary Wright, our lead contact in the Folger Shakespearean Library and Theater negotiations that led to our historic partnership with the revered institution, an alliance which continued to bear fruit for a number of years.

Geneva

Nothing prepared me for the munificent comment made from the platform in the Russell House Ballroom at the late 1980s conference on European Affairs by then-U.S. Vice President George H.W. Bush. As his words resonated, I sat back and fully assimilated what he was saying, realizing that we had been preparing to warrant such words since I arrived:

"If this keeps up, America may get its own equivalent of Vienna or Geneva, right here in Columbia."

"This" was our purposeful and dedicated programmatic initiatives to stimulate international dialogue and cultivate diplomatic exchange.

The University of South Carolina generally, and sometimes the President's House in particular, became an incubator for introductions of cultures and political points of view and the melding of influential individuals who forged new connections and reached new conclusions while on our campus.

When Vice President Bush spoke here for the first time he probably had no idea that plans were being made, even then, for the Byrnes International Center to host an International Monetary Fund Conference that would draw 20 of the nation's top financial leaders to the University.

In a column in *The State* newspaper, business writer Fred Monk wrote: "If the 'Carolina' name isn't getting well known in international circles, it's not USC's fault. USC has been, in recent years, a crossroads for presidents, prime ministers, foreign ministers and other decision-makers in international politics and business."

Some of the deals and agreements that came out of those conferences originated in our living room.

One evening, during a reception in our home given for our newly-formed International Advisory Board, I noticed Larry Eagleburger, then U.S. Deputy Secretary of State, in deep conversation with Lord Peter Carrington, a former United Kingdom Secretary of State for Foreign Affairs who also had been former High Commissioner to Australia. The two were stand-

Joining us on the Horseshoe welcoming guests from the Republic of China is former Lt. Governor Mike Daniel who accompanied the USC delegation to China in 1981.

The Chinese Ambassador and his wife read The Gamecock article covering their historic visit in the early '80s.

ing in front of the non-functioning fireplace. When the seriousness of their talk gave way to smiles and shoulder clapping, Eagleburger turned to the assembled crowd and said, "May I introduce to you the next Secretary General of NATO!"

While serving as Secretary of State, Henry Kissinger traveled frequently to the Middle East in quest of a lasting peace, he was generally accompanied by his principal deputy, Larry Eagleburger. Over the years, both of these foreign policy giants became close friends of USC, playing significant parts in the emerging international role assumed by the University. And they seemed to have great fun doing so – often at the expense of one another.

Eagleburger loved telling the story of one very late arrival in a large Middle East city; both were very tired and eager for rest. However, piercing sounds of the regular Islamic call to prayer emanated from minarets across the city! Dr. Kissinger directed his deputy to see what could be done to silence the prayer-beckoning chants. Recognizing the futility of any such effort, Larry reminded the Secretary of State of its likely failure, and the impropriety of such a request.

Ashraf Ghorbal was one of those whose relational regard for us bore fruit. In addition to his pivotal post, at least where we were concerned, he held many others. When he retired he was Dean of the Diplomatic Corps in

Mike Daniel, right, joined me as our Chinese hosts welcomed us to their extraordinary country. "Gam Bei!"

Staying warm was a priority when we visited China. Trustee Chairman Markley Dennis, right, traveled with us.

BYRNES INTERNATIONAL CENTER ADVISORY BOARD

On the Byrnes International Center Advisory Board, our international contingent included not only Lord Carrington of the United Kingdom, but also a Who's Who list of others:

Prime Minister Eugenia Charles of Dominica

Viscount Étienne Davignon, Vice President of the European Community

Prime Minister Malcolm Fraser of Australia

Ashraf Ghorbal, Egyptian Ambassador to the U.S.

The Right Honorable Dr. John Gilbert, a member of the British Parliament and U.K. Minister of Transport and later Secretary of State for Defense

Sir Nicholas Henderson, British Ambassador to the U.S.

His Excellency Yoshiro Okawara, Japanese Ambassador to Australia and later to the U.S.

The Right Honorable Lord James Prior, British Secretary of State for Northern Ireland

Elie A. Salem, Lebanese Deputy Prime Minister and Minister of Foreign Affairs

Prime Minister Edward Seaga of Jamaica

Güenther Van Well, West German Ambassador to the United States

The Honorable Henri Simonet, Belgian Vice President of the Commission of the European Community

Zhang Wenjin, Chinese Ambassador to Pakistan and later to the United States

Lawrence Eagleburger, former Secretary of the United States

William Brock, former Secretary of Labor

Andreas Van Agt, former Prime Minister of the Netherlands and Ambassador of the European Community to the United States

Many became great friends – to me and to Carolina. The intrinsic worth of these relationships was value added for the University.

Washington. He served for several years on the Byrnes International Center board.

One day early in his relationship with Carolina, he and I were walking across the Horseshoe to the President's House. The campus was nearly empty for a semester break. I saw only one student seated on a bench across the way, studying. I asked a security officer to encourage the student to meet our guest. The student obliged and walked over to us. When Ghorbal asked him where he was from, the student answered: "Cairo, Egypt." Ghorbal was flabbergasted! He said, "Jim, this has to be a set up! What else could this be? An Egyptian student is the only student on campus, just when I am walking across the Horseshoe?" I assured him I did not pre-arrange

Malcolm Fraser was a serious guy. But he also could be a lot of fun. Before his departure from a visit to Carolina, as Prime Minister of Australia, we presented him with a hand-made Carolina rifle for his hunting in Australia. He assured us he would have no trouble getting it through Australian customs.

Jim Kuhlman, left, and I welcome Budimir Loncar, Ambassador from Yugoslavia (whose friendship was very helpful in basketball recruiting). Gov. Dick Riley is on the right.

it – it was pure coincidence, but it certainly proved how successful USC had become at attracting international students.

Later, Carolyn entered the Kennedy bedroom, where she had directed Ghorbal for prayer, to find him on his prayer rug facing west instead of east. She suggested he might want to correct that and face east, properly to Mecca. “If God can’t find me, that’s too bad,” he countered.

In July, 1987, a conference on U.S. – Japanese trade relations was hosted by USC and the Japan Foundation, presented through the prestigious Keidanren in Tokyo. That fall, USC also sponsored a conference on technology, education and human resources in the Caribbean on the Carolina campus. It was former Japanese Ambassador to the U.S. Yoshio Okawara who encouraged the University to be a part of this conference. A major advisor to Keidanren, Yoshio certainly became a good friend of ours. As avid golfers, both he and his wife Mitsuko played as many South Carolina golf courses as possible.

Shortly after that, also on the Columbia campus, a conference on U.S. – Japanese business opportunities was held in partnership with Clemson University and MUSC. USC's presentation was given entirely in Japanese, which both surprised and delighted our Japanese guests. One of our MIBS students told the story that while studying in Tokyo his wife had a baby and they stamped its bottom with "Made in Japan," which the business crowd loved!

In the mid-'80s, at the request of good friends in Washington, D.C., USC was asked to help welcome Shintaro Abé, Trade Minister of Japan, by presenting him with an honorary degree and welcoming him with a ceremony on the Columbia campus. We heartily agreed and hosted the awarding at a ceremony in the President's House Gardens. The current Prime Minister of Japan, Shinzo Abé, is the son of the man we honored in the '80s.

The U.S. Century Foundation, which arose from a conference at USC in 1985, focused on the Future of the Atlantic and Pacific communities and their shared desire to stimulate private initiatives to strengthen and renew ties among their partner nations. Sir David Wills raised $4.5 million for the fund, and President Reagan endorsed it the following year – all for the purpose of increasing collaboration and coordination among those nations, and bypassing U.S. and U.K. organizations.

By 1980, we had established the James F. Byrnes International Center, appointing professor Kuhlman as first Director. The Center became the home office of the North American International Studies Association under Kuhlman's Executive Directorship. That organization grew from a few hundred scholars in the U.S. to a few thousand scholars from across the golobe. The University of South Carolina clearly had made a mark on the global map.

On campus, we nurtured the number one ranked Masters in International Business Studies of the College of Business Administration. The Earth Sciences and Resources Institute was moved into the Byrnes Center and achieved

Esmat Meguid, third from left, and his wife are welcomed to Carolina. Meguid became president of the Arab League; at the time of his visit he was Egypt's representative to the United Nations. The Ambassador was the featured speaker at the annual Inter-fraternity and PanHellenic Banquet on the campus.

Lord Peter Carrington demonstrates the "Cock-A-Doodle-Do!" cry of the Carolina Gamecock.

"Can you hear Carrington up there?" Lord Peter Carrington and Malcolm Fraser, both respected leaders in the British Commonwealth, joined in advocating the end of apartheid in the Union of South Africa.

global recognition with the support of local business icon Wilbur Smith. The Department of Government and International Studies rose to prominence in its field. In Public Health, in Marine Sciences, in Physics and many other disciplines, USC's reputation grew globally. The Byrnes Center undertook the direction of Governor Riley's new program Leadership South Carolina, providing current issues program for fifty leading young Carolinians each year, with a strong emphasis on international concerns.

In 1986, the Byrnes Center coordinated a conference on three Western Hemisphere countries transitioning from military to democratic rule: Argentina, Uruguay and Chile. Financial support came from the United States Information Agency (USIA). Professor Morris Blachman, a USC expert in Latin American Affairs, planned the conference which explored what the scholarly community understood about the transition.

Such a role reinforced Carolina's reputation as an institution intellectually and logistically capable of managing major international conferences and its commitment to bringing about discussion of important global issues.

Long before climate change had emerged as an issue of global importance, Dr. Doug Williams of the University's Department of Geological Sciences reported on the Lake Baikal Project, in which we were heavily involved in the Soviet Union. We knew then it was the largest and deepest freshwater lake on the planet; it contains one-fifth of the world's fresh water and, at its base, some five kilometers of sediment that has developed over millions of years. Drilling into that lakebed would establish a long-term documentation of climate change. Again, USC was ahead of its time in participating in some of the most important scientific issues in the world.

Along with Williams' presentation, Dr. Gordon B. Smith, Professor of Government and International Studies, reported the planned expansion of a modest exchange program with Kazan State University, one of Russia's pre-eminent universities, situated on the Volga River in Kazan. The exchange program, funded in 1988 by the United States Agency for International Development (USAID), aligned the University with Dartmouth College, the University of Wisconsin-Madison and the University of South Carolina.

To follow up on the 1984 Caribbean Basin Initiative, which had drawn President Reagan to address the group, we had begun planning a second Caribbean and Central American Heads of State meeting for Columbia, 1991. No other institution was assuming that role.

On a related matter, our College of Journalism and Mass Communication had begun a small-scale program to engage Caribbean journalists in a program exchange. Under the leadership of Dr. Kent Seidel, the stated goal was achieved: establishing USC as the center for training Caribbean journalists – starting with hosting radio journalists from Belize, Costa Rica, St. Vincent, Haiti and Guyana. The first group of 32 from the Caribbean had arrived on campus in January of that year,

At a retirement party hosted by the University to honor Ambassador Ghorbal's retirement from the Egyptian Embassy, Associate Justice Lewis F. Powell of the U.S. Supreme Court, left, was among those who brought best wishes to our close friend.

Edward Seaga, Prime Minister of Jamaica, and Andreas Van Agt, Prime Minister of the Netherlands, at the European Security Conference.

Japanese Ambassador Okawara is congratulated at his USC hosted D.C. retirement dinner by U.S. Chief Justice Warren Burger.

and students were being placed at University System campuses to pursue associate degrees in management and technical training. This was part of the Byrnes Center's Comparative Association of State for Scholarships (CAAS), a national program administered by Georgetown University for USAID.

We also were hosting a third event at Longstreet Theater, focusing on the economic reform process in Western Europe. Typical of Byrnes Center events, there was a panel discussion. This one was hosted by Paul Drake of PBS News and was composed of: Lord Peter Carrington; former U.S. Senator, Foreign Trade Ambassador and Secretary of Labor William Brock; European Economic Community (E.E.C.) Ambassador Andreas Van Agt; and USC Professor Jeff Arpan. The discussion addressed the liberalization of Eastern and Central Europe on the pace of reform in Western Europe.

A fourth event set for that fall in Washington, D.C. was planned to concentrate on the opportunities for American financial service companies in the new Europe.

Considered at that last meeting before my departure from USC on July 1, 1990, were a number of proposals that would have involved institutions in Yugoslavia, Bulgaria, Czechoslovakia, Hungary and Romania.

In just over a decade, the extraordinary work of the Byrnes Center and people throughout the entire system had put South Carolina and the University front and center of important dialog, practical research, and student and faculty exchange programs. Foreign and national leaders on our campus, here to do important work, attracted global media attention and respect among the nations of the world. Following my resignation at Carolina, my successor closed the Byrnes International Center, and its many planned functions for the 21st century did not occur.

I was generally sure I handled myself well during most of these high-visibility occasions – except for one experience in England. Carolyn and I along with Lord and Lady Peter Carrington were lunching at a London hotel. When time came for dessert, the waiter asked if we cared for some sorbet. I said, "No thank you, but have you any sherbet?" Carolyn leaned over and discretely said to her small-town Illinois partner: "Jim, sorbet IS sherbet!"

Despite rumors that Eagleburger and I were joined at the hip, it was not the case, as proven by this photo. However, he was a good enough friend to make a special trip to Columbia to help Bill Foster successfully recruit basketball players from Yugoslavia. Having been the Ambassador to Yugoslavia during the Tito years, Eagleburger was fluent in Serbo-Croation, the country's official language.

Larry Eagleburger became a fixture at our podium during his years of friendship with the University, culminating in his service as Chairman of the International Advisory Board and the Byrnes International Center, before and after serving as U.S. Secretary of State.

Brent Scowcroft, left, National Security Advisor under President Ford, also served in that capacity under President George H. W. Bush, right. Scowcroft enjoyed a good laugh with Bush.

Vice President George H. W. Bush, Admiral Scowcroft, and Lord Peter Carrington joke: "Well, I can't think of a better place to be the Geneva of the West than right here: smack dab in the heart of the ole South! Can you?"

The Fourth Estate

My early observations were that the University had been camera shy; that is, the institution had not been a gleam in the media's eye nearly often enough. Instinct told me we could not achieve our potential without the media's amplification and dissemination – even glorification would have suited me well. To become a twinkle in the media's eye, though, we first needed to do more things to elicit that twinkle. So we did.

Walter Cronkite, anchor of the *CBS Evening News* for well over a decade, had accepted the University's invitation to address the annual luncheon for initiates into Phi Beta Kappa. Unfortunately, the day of his scheduled speech, the United States' attempt to free hostages in Iran was aborted. Quite naturally, Cronkite was tied up. Despite his hectic reporting schedule, Steve Beckham from the USC President's office was able to set up a radio link to the Russell House where the luncheon was being held. His broadcast reached a very excited audience via closed circuit.

Cronkite's generous spirit showed forth a few months later when he ran me down while I was traveling in Chicago to tell me he had not forgotten he owed me a speech. "Great! Thanks!" I said, "How would our May commencement suit you?" He agreed and came. Graduates and their families loved it. His voice was one that most of us had become accustomed to hearing over the years as he was the spokesman for so many iconic events: the assassination of President John F. Kennedy, America's Space Program and the Civil Rights Movement, among others. When Cronkite came to USC, he sat in the library of the President's House and told us stories from his decades as a working reporter in journalism. At some point during his pontification, his wife, Betsy, gave him the hook, telling him – and everyone within earshot that evening – he may be the most trusted man in America, but its time to put a sock in it. Cronkite had been labeled as such for his straightforward reporting on CBS Evening News during two of America's most tumultuous decades.

Jim Lehrer who, with Canadian-American television reporter and novelist Robin MacNeil, anchored National Public Radio's *MacNeil/Lehrer Report* as early as 1975, first came to USC in 1979-80 to moderate the Republi-

As the University gained a foothold in international matters, we were able to afford Carolina friends introductions to leaders of note. Louis Sossamon, an USC alumnus and long-time editor of the Gaffney Ledger*, left, meets Tom Adams, Prime Minister of Barbados, in 1984.*

Long-time CBS news anchor Walter Cronkite, right, accepts an honorary degree from the University of South Carolina. He inscribed his book to me: "To Jim Holderman, with the best in lasting friendship. - Walter Cronkite"

can Presidential debates. His handling of that broadcast from Longstreet Theater, catalyzed future requests for him to moderate important panels around the country. He and MacNeil returned as visiting lecturers in our College of Journalism classes and inspired our students to look for both the big picture and the smallest picture, be correct, and exemplify integrity. For this effort on their part, they received considerable attention on prominent pages of the *New York Times* and other dailies. Jim suffered a heart attack in the late '80s and I had the audacity to wire him to say I was surprised to know that he had a heart, but was pleased to hear he was improving. If I had listened to his advice early in my troubles with the press, I might have avoided many problems. He counseled me to give the media what they sought; I thought I knew better. As it turns out, I didn't!

Some media and legislators thought I was going too fast and too furious.

Ted Koppel, British-American broadcast journalist and long-time anchor of *ABC's Nightline*, had accepted our invitation to come to Carolina to receive an honorary degree. He was en route when travel hang-ups intervened, and the processional had settled into the Coliseum without him. From the podium I had begun to tell the Eleanor Roosevelt story. She had been invited to speak at a commencement, was introduced, made it to the podium, then turned and went back to her seat. The college

Our distinguished lecturer Jim Lehrer, left, well known for his moderating political debates and his long-running The MacNeil-Lehrer News Hour *on PBS, meets USC Student Body President Glenn German at one of our events in Washington, D.C.*

Jim Lehrer, far left, is the moderator for this watershed event in Carolina's history. On February 28, 1980, Republican candidates for U.S. President debated in our Longstreet Theater. In addition to Ronald Reagan, center, candidates were Howard Baker, John Connolly, and George H.W. Bush.

The retirement dinner for Ghorbal included Katharine Graham, publisher of The Washington Post *and* Newsweek *magazine and one of news media's most formidable executives. Here she has best wishes for our friend Ashraf Ghorbal as he retires from his diplomatic post as Egyptian Ambassador to the United States. On the left is Ben Bradlee, editor of* The Washington Post.

president went over to her and said, "Won't you say a few words?" She said, "Not today." Just as I was trying to get us out of hot water by invoking what humor I could muster, Koppel showed up and was ushered immediately to the podium. I started breathing again.

Katharine Graham was not a guest on our campus, but accepted our invitation to attend the Washington retirement party for our friend, Egyptian Ambassador Ashraf Ghorbal. To have, among our guests, one of the most powerful members of the media was a great complement to the University. In fact, we were continually told that our visibility in Washington was growing dramatically. We felt that couldn't hurt us, and it certainly didn't.

Back in South Carolina, our activities and initiatives brought banks of photographers and teams of reporters to our campus on a regular basis. The media's reasons for being at Carolina ranged from giving classroom lectures to capturing coverage live.

There are many reasons I won't forget the day Steve Beckham had to tell WIS-TV reporter Lou Fontana to cut off his camera. Fontana was set up right outside of Osborne and was broadcasting, live, as a distraught faculty member was inside my office demanding the tenure he said he had been promised. This clearly disturbed assistant professor of philosophy was watching

Seeing banks of photographers warmed my heart on the day of the Pope's visit. But not always!

the scenario unfold on the TV in my office. The upset man demanded that WIS-TV personality Joe Pinner be contacted to negotiate on his behalf. We put the man in touch with Pinner by phone. The disgruntled man's attorney soon replaced Joe. I was not in the office; SLED and Campus Security would not allow me to return. The day ended very badly with the faculty member taking his own life at my desk.

Quite generally, managing the media was a challenge I delegated trustingly to my long-time friend and able ally Chris Vlahoplus. I armed myself against the media's volleys with my own preferred media tool: the telephone. To assure I was never more than an arm's length away from what was happening, we had 17 phones on four lines in the President's House and several more in my Osborne office. It was not unusual for a phone to ring in the middle of the night. Such calls seldom conveyed good news.

It is still stunning to recall the telephone report I got telling me that Gamecocks Football Coach Jim Morrison had died, most unexpectedly, while at his ground-level offices in Williams-Brice Stadium. The next call was from WIS-TV asking if I had a replacement for Morrison in mind. I scoffed.

One night the ringing of the phone warned: "Mister President, you better not go out your back door," delivered in a throaty, menacing voice. I suspected it was some kind of routine campus occurrence but, out of an abundance of caution, I called the campus police and asked them to check it out. Then my curiosity got the best of me. I went downstairs in my robe and watched as a campus policeman focused the beam of his flashlight on a pile of clothing and blankets. When the officer gently nudged the pile with his toe, out crawled a very inebriated and naked Carolina student who had no idea where he was – but he knew he was in trouble. Relieved and amused, I told the policeman to get the young man dressed and take him back to his dorm. No harm done.

Just another night on campus!

Hitting the Half-Century Mark

Celebration of my 50th birthday was something of a crucible, career-wise. The event was held at one of Washington, D.C.'s finest hotels, a property where I stayed when I was in the nation's capital on University business. Gathered around me that evening were people whose lives had touched mine, along with others I admired but barely knew such as:

U.S. Senator J. William Fulbright from Arkansas
Chief Justice of the United States Warren Burger
U.S. Senator Strom Thurmond
U.S. Senator Fritz Hollings
U.S. Senator Mark Hatfield of Oregon
Hon. Sir Roy Denman, Ambassador of the EEC to the United States
Hon. Sir Oliver Wright, Ambassador of the United Kingdom to the United States
Hon. Edward J. Meese, Attorney General of the United States
Bill J. Timmons, former assistant to three Presidents of the United States
Hon. William Brock, U.S. Secretary of Labor
Lane Kirkland, President of AFL-CIO

In these cases, the guests had been invited by someone with ties to the University. At times that evening, I felt I was a guest on This Is Your Life, *a television show popular during my youth, because most of the attendees at the party were touchstones representing countless projects, issues, or campaigns I had engaged in sometime prior to that milestone in my career and life.*

The party was nearly cancelled. The Challenger Space Shuttle had exploded earlier that day – January 28, 1986. There was a hush and a shudder around the world, especially in Washington. When organizers began trying to reach those on the guest list, they found many were already en route to D.C. and would not know to amend their travel arrangements. So we went ahead.

Naturally, the tragedy was the prevailing topic of conversation throughout the evening. But after a pensive start, talk gradually found other topics. Leading the banter were some of the most effective conversationalists on Capitol Hill. Bill Timmons probably led that pack. It was Bill, former assistant to three presidents, who had put me in line for the American Red Cross appointment, with rank of Ambassador. The appointment as chairman of the U.S. National Commission for

Chief Justice Warren Burger was flanked here by former Governor Robert E. McNair and U.S. Senator Strom Thurmond.

George Haley, left, and Jonathan Davidson shared a pleasant moment with U.S. Senator Mark Hatfield of Oregon.

UNESCO came through the efforts of Timmons and close friend Deputy Secretary of State, Larry Eagleburger.

Our genial hosts were Marshall Coyne and Bob Woody. Marshall Coyne, who for many years had made the Inside the Beltway property at 1177 Fifteenth Street, N.W. the accommodation of choice for discerning travelers – from presidents to heads of state, diplomats and other headliners.

Marshall oversaw a loyal staff, many with service spanning my adult years; they all rendered impeccable service. I counted both Bob and Marshall among my very close friends. Marshall was a connoisseur of anything associated with the hotel and also was an avid collector of Chinese art. His finesse helped make the birthday party a refined occasion in spite of the pall that hung over the nation at the loss of the Challenger and its crew. Bob Woody was one of my best friends; he served as USC's D.C. counsel during all of my tenure. Because of his background in the oil business, he was especially instrumental in our success in raising money for the Swearingen Engineering Center.

Bob Woody

It was Bob who coined the phrase, the "Gee-Whiz" factor, to describe the style of my administration at USC.

Sir Roy Denman, EEC Ambassador to the U.S., and U.S. Chief Justice Warren Burger were among guests at the 50th birthday party in my honor at The Madison Hotel in Washington, D.C. on January 28th, 1986.

As I often did, I checked in with former presidential assistant and respected D.C. lobbyist Bill Timmons.

Chief Justice Warren Burger was welcomed by Marshall Coyne, who made The Madison Hotel run like a well-oiled top.

Good friends U.S. Senator Mark Hatfield and Chief Justice Warren Burger engaged in warm conversation.

Staff assistants chatted with Chief Justice Warren Burger.

Co-host Marshall Coyne, left, welcomed U.K. Ambassador Sir Oliver Wright and former Governor Robert McNair.

The Madison Hotel's owner Marshall Coyne visited with U.S. Senator J. William Fulbright.

Golden Friends

Before arriving at USC late in the summer of 1977, I had been privileged to meet, shake hands with, work with, and get to know some very interesting, sometimes very influential folks. The overall benefit of many of these associations gave me grounding and continuity – and helped me lead Carolina forward. On a more personal note, my Rolodex swelled in South Carolina, but more importantly, I made some Golden Friends.

Three years after Pope John Paul II's visit to Columbia, Joseph Cardinal Bernardin, who had been the single most influential person in the scheduling of the papal visit to Columbia, wrote about his feelings that early afternoon in St. Pater's Church at the Pope's first stop. "I was born only a few blocks from the Church; I was baptized, confirmed, made my first confession and received Holy Communion for the first time there. As a young boy of six years, I witnessed the funeral rites of my father. And later, as a student at St. Peter's School and as an altar boy, I got to know, intimately, the priests and religious leaders who contributed so much to the parish's character ... my most emotional return to St. Peter's occurred on September 11, 1987, when I walked with Pope John Paul II down the middle aisle as he greeted and blessed worshippers who had packed the church. I had walked down that aisle many times as an altar boy, but this time was different. History was being made, and I was proud to be a part of it."

Joseph Cardinal Bernardin was a dear friend. A native of Columbia, he had attended pre-med classes at Carolina before entering the seminary. Once ordained, he was a parish priest in Columbia and Charleston, Auxiliary Bishop of Atlanta and Archbishop of Cincinnati. He held that position when I first met him. He was named Archbishop of Chicago in 1982, and a year later Pope John Paul II, his close friend, made him a Cardinal.

I like to recall an evening with him at the Madison Hotel in Washington, D.C. I had been asked by U.S. Secretary of Labor Bill Brock to set up a meeting with Bernardin, whose numerous responsibilities included service on the Catholic committee to study moral guidelines attendant to atomic weapons of mass destruction. We were given a private dining room in which to hold this cloistered discussion about nuclear armament. One of the select few seated around the table that night was William P. Clark, Reagan's national security advisor who

Federal Judge Matthew Perry, right, and his wife Hallie.

My oldest daughter Betsy, like all of our daughters, got to know dignitaries like Joseph Cardinal Bernardin quite well.

previously had been Superior Court Judge in California. All evening Bill deferred unctuously to Bernardin, even refusing to leave until Joe departed ahead of him. I took particular note of this behavior since I knew Bill had attended Jesuit schools.

Carolyn and I hosted a formal Capstone dinner in the Cardinal's honor to welcome him home and afford an opportunity for his many Catholic family and friends to greet him as the new Cardinal Archbishop of Chicago. Just before the dinner, I went to see him in the Kennedy bedroom and complimented him on his festive robes of black and crimson red. (To me they read Garnet and Black!)

He responded lightly: "Ah, Jimmy, when you've got it, flaunt it!" This was a rare (and private) expression for a man known for his modesty. His mother had told him on the day of his installation as Archbishop, "Joe, just don't smile too much." He was a tremendous intellect and an international force. If he had lived, many think he might have been the first American Pope. He served brilliantly as Chairman of USC's National Advisory Committee and was influential in assuring that Pope John Paul II would visit Columbia in 1987.

To my understanding, the Cardinal made only one error as far as the University of South Carolina was concerned: he sentenced himself to life by telling me he would serve as Chairman of the Advisory Council as long as I wanted him to. Only outside factors could save him from that lengthy but uncertain fate.

At an informal dinner at his official residence, he asked my good friend Arthur Wirtz, the wealthy realtor who owned the Chicago Bulls, Blackhawks and the Chicago Stadium as well as the American Furniture Mart: "What do you think the Archbishop's residence on State Parkway is worth?" Without hesitation, Wirtz responded: "Probably around $28 million." A Catholic witness to the conversation said: "That sure beats Bingo!" Bernardin replied (almost Sotto Voce): "It sure as hell does!" What a prince of a man, one of the most impressive people I have ever known.

The same can be said for James Michener, with whom I became acquainted in my UNESCO activities. My treasured friend, Lyn Nofziger, who had been President Reagan's principal political advisor in California and at the White House, Jim and I were on the same panel along with a very special lady for whom I felt immediate rapport and affection: Ursula Meese, the wife of U.S. Attorney General Ed Meese.

Jim Michener, the author of such classics as: *Tales of the South Pacific, The Source, Centennial, Texas, Hawaii, Caravan,* and many more, became a fascinating friend. On those occasions, when we were together, he was, not surprising-

Mary Alice and Pat Patterson were the residents of the President's House just prior to our family moving in. Pat had a long history with the University before becoming president. Here they were chatting with former board chairman Othniel Wienges, left.

ly, quite compelling. I tried to persuade him to come to Carolina for a commencement and honorary degree, but he was always so deeply involved in the incomparable research he would do for each and every book. At one dinner, I recall, at a Mexico City UNESCO meeting on Cultural Affairs, Jim Michener revealed, with considerable modesty, the totals of taxes he had paid on income for his books. While I will not even consider breaking the confidence of that conversation years ago, I will say that a number of third world countries could fund their total governments on the figure.

Lord Carrington visited Carolina three or four times and remains a good friend. He appears quite regularly on the evening news, often heading missions for the United Nations in Bosnia and South Africa. His sense of humor is the best of British wit, as evidenced, at least in part, by his collection of epitaphs. Peter shared a number of them when Carolyn and I spent several days at the Carrington country manor, where Peter is the Lord, and Iona the Lady. One of his favorite epitaphs is found on a tombstone in Belfast, Northern Ireland:

Here lies Patrick O'Boyle
Brutally murdered by the British
While peacefully lying in ambush.

I was not the only one who looked up to Brad Jergenson, one-time varsity basketball star and subsequently one of our staff.

Caroline McKissick Belser Dial, left, often showed me more of what Carolina could be.

The Carringtons were most kind when they made their first visit to South Carolina. We hosted a large luncheon in their honor, and he delivered a major speech on the emerging European community, cautioning us not to expect miracles from a society which would be characterized by English cuisine, French driving habits, German humor, and Italian punctuality!

The extraordinarily accomplished USC concert choir presented a repertoire of great pieces, thoughtfully dedicating one number to Lady Carrington, which she graciously acknowledged. After an encore, and then a second, everyone was ready to wrap it up when Carolyn said to me loud enough for the microphone to pick up, "Jim, have them do the one that they've just learned the words to." I demurred, but Arpad Darazs, our superior choir director, heard my first lady's request. The choir broke, almost immediately, into the familiar music, and until then, most unfamiliar words. We concluded a luncheon of tribute to the British Foreign Secretary and his wife, belonging to a titled family that reached back hundreds of years, well before the American Revolution, by offering "The Stars and Stripes Forever." The little known lyrics of the second verse erased any doubt about the mighty tune's meaning. Peter and Iona smiled politely and went home.

Malcolm Fraser of the "get in line" abuse group served as Prime Minister of Australia, and is a bear of a man: over 6' 6", and usually quite gentle. On his first USC visit, when he was P.M., he was honored at a luncheon on the second floor of the President's house. At the close of the meal, the student waitress did not know the lid of the silver pot was unattached, so, when she poured his coffee, the lid fell off into the Prime Ministers' cup, splashing hot coffee into Mr. Fraser's lap. Here is the mark of the man: he put his arm around her waist and said to the young lady, whose eyes were already brimming with tears, "This is a moment you will never forget; nor will I. Tell your grandchildren about it."

Later that same day, as our Australian guests were settling in at the house, the wife of the Australian Prime Minister told Carolyn in a subtle voice that the toilet adjacent to their room was not working. Tamie Fraser volunteered to fix the "john." "I do it every Christmas at home when the plumbers won't come." Tamie Fraser: a neat woman!

Some of my very special friends are, not surprisingly, from the Academic Community. Two of these were Father Ted Hesburgh, President Emeritus of Notre Dame, and his great associate for 35 years at Notre Dame, Father Ned Joyce, Executive Vice President for Academic Affairs and a native of Spartanburg, South Carolina.

My first meeting with Father Ted occurred in 1975 when President Ford visited Notre Dame. I recall that the President brought the huge audience at Notre Dame to uproarious laughter when he reported that as he had deplaned at the South Bend airport that morning, he asked the first person he saw how

Former House Speaker Sol Blatt, center, became one of my most trusted allies. Sol was succeeded by Speaker Rex Carter, not pictured, and Speaker Ramon Schwarz, left.

Glenn German, president of the USC Columbia Student Body, sat down to play the piano in the President's House. Now he is a Hollywood screenwriter.

Guy Lipscomb, Jr., left, revered alumnus, entrepreneur and artist, talks with Richard Shafto, whose formative leadership remains discernable throughout WIS's broadcasting reach.

to get to Notre Dame University. The man said he had no idea. Then, the President reported, "I found out later that the man was Father Hesburgh".

Similar humor about me circulated in the Carolina Community. A former Dean of Students, Marsha Duncan, an outstanding dean, used the following lines: "What is the difference between God and Jim Holderman? God is everywhere and Jim Holderman is everywhere but the University of South Carolina." My retort was: "Another difference between God and me is that God forgives Marsha."

I was first introduced to Larry Eagleburger aboard the Carolina plane flying to a conference of the International Studies Association. USC was soon to become the international headquarters for the ISA. Although neither of us would admit it, we became good friends on that trip, as evidenced by our next encounter. Several weeks later, I attended a small and informal dinner party at the British Embassy. My friend, British Ambassador Sir Nicholas Henderson, included me for the event. My stressed sense of confidence was convincing me that I did not belong. The dinner party was

Ben and Henriette Morris chatted with Henry Kissinger. Ben was the last family publisher of The State *newspaper.*

Federal Judge Matthew Perry, second from right, and his wife, Hallie, conversed with Federal Judge Ross Anderson and his wife, Dot.

Retired House Speaker Sol Blatt, left, and his son, Federal Judge Sol Blatt, were treasured friends of the University of South Carolina.

comprised of twelve or so recognizable personalities, and was meant to honor another good friend, Jim Prior, Prime Minister Thatcher's Secretary of State for Employment. His U.S. counterpart, Bill Brock, Secretary of Labor, and Katharine Graham of the *Washington Post/NEWSWEEK* were there, as well as several others in that league. Across from me there was an empty place awaiting a tardy guest. In a few minutes, with a suitably conspicuous entrance, Larry Eagleburger arrived and was seated. He looked around the room without giving me an instant's recognition and seemed to be ignoring me.

I told myself that the S.O.B. doesn't even remember me, and when I looked up, he handed me his place card. I thought this guy was reminding me who he was; instead, I flipped over the card and read the message he had jotted inside: "Holderman, what are you doing slumming it here?" Still funny to this day, if only to me!

Henry Kissinger has said to me on several occasions that Larry has built a career mimicking and imitating Henry, who was, off and on, Larry's boss. Dr. Kissinger has indicated that over the phone, Larry could sound more like Henry than Henry does.

Mayor Kirkman Finlay, center, was always alert to ways the City of Columbia and the University could strengthen their ties. At right is Güenther Van Well, German Ambassador to the United States.

Pat Bowman with Mary Kay Burke (Bowman) and me. Pat was held hostage by a distraught, non-tenured professor in my office over the course of several hours before being released safely.

Governor Dick Riley, center, conferred with USC Provost Frank Borkowski.

Danny Kaye met General William Childs Westmoreland. Danny was internationally acclaimed as an international supporter of UNICEF, and was speaker at our May commencement in 1985.

South Carolina's U.S. Sen. Fritz Hollings joined me at a commencement dinner late in my tenure at Carolina.

When Ashraf Ghorbal, the dean of the Washington diplomatic corps and warm friend of USC, was preparing to retire and return to Egypt, USC hosted a dinner for him and his gracious wife Amahl in the nation's capitol. Among the very distinguished guests was David Rockefeller, scion of his own extraordinary family, and a very welcome guest and close friend of Ambassador Ghorbal.

"I Had Gifts ... But I Gave Them All Away"

Even I would have shrunk from attempting glibness on an occasion in which Billy Graham was opening a Crusade at Williams Brice Stadium in the summer of 1986. Following a series of speakers who had presented gifts of welcome to the Reverend Billy Graham, it just came out! I blurted, "I had gifts ... but I have given them all away!" The crowd, which had some knowledge of my penchant for "gifting," did more than snicker. Many, too many, guffawed.

As part of my acclimation to Southern culture, I made it a standard practice to give a gift as meaningful as possible to guests who graced us with their presence and interest in the University. In time, that habit turned against me. I never attempted to reconcile the monetary value of those mementoes with the gifts of money, connections, and considerations that came back to the University. Reciprocity was not my aim; hospitality and the development of long-term relationships absolutely were.

What memento do you give to someone who has everything he could possibly need? On Ronald Reagan's first presidential visit to our campus in 1983, we presented him with a Steuben glass Excalibur. He feigned pulling the sword out – unsuccessfully. He couldn't, so he asked me if it was meant to be that way or if it was it a joke. I wondered, "Could it be that Arthur's legendary sword is resisting him?" We all smiled as he easily removed the sword from the stone!

As we succeeded in attracting high-profile guests to campus, the practice of giving a gift of some kind became something of a hallmark for my administration. I wanted the gifts to be as meaningful as possible. A good example of that attention to detail is a Lincoln document we acquired as a gift for the President of the Dominican Republic, Salvador Jorgé Blanco. The artifact's date was the same date as his visit to Springfield, Illinois – although a very different year. There were times when such convergence of detail and circumstance were planned, while others turned out to be happenstance. This was one of the latter.

Glass by Steuben, Boehm porcelains, Audubon prints, autographed historical documents, original art work, and first editions went home with influential guests visiting us from across the state, the country, and even the globe.

Although he jokingly failed several times, President Ronald Reagan was able to pull the sword Excalibur out of the stone, a gift he was given on his visit to the USC Horseshoe in September 1983. The tradition of hosting dignitaries began in 1825 with the Marquis de Lafayette's visit to the South Carolina College campus and continued through the visit of Pope John Paul II in September 1987.

Many guests received Boehm glass sculptures of the State's Bird, the Carolina wren. Only one guest ever returned hers, fearing acceptance of a gift would give the appearance that she was being "bought." I still doubt that an innocent Carolina wren would have been capable of corrupting the wife of a state leader.

Even some of my harshest critics acknowledge that I "put USC on the map." I DO love to hear that!

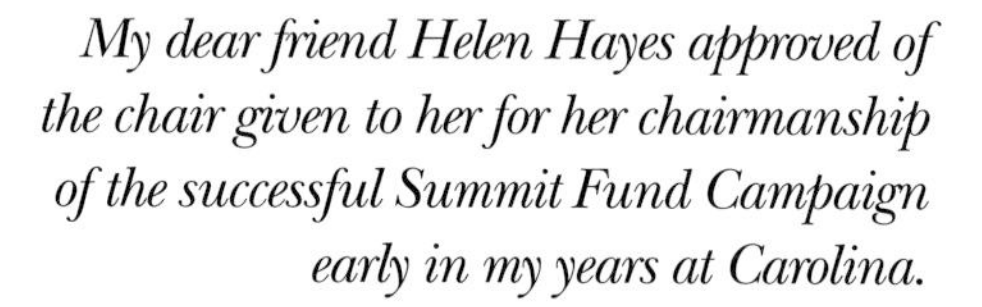

My dear friend Helen Hayes approved of the chair given to her for her chairmanship of the successful Summit Fund Campaign early in my years at Carolina.

To help Dominican Republic President Salvador Jorgé Blanco remember his visit to the University of South Carolina, we gave him an historic Lincoln document, coincidentally dated the same day as his visit to Springfield, Illinois – although with well over a century between dates.

Afterword

As a student once informed us, the University of South Carolina "used to have the reputation that 'if you have a driver's license, you can get in.'" To put it rather mildly, that image no longer holds true. Under the leadership of James Holderman, Carolina's (the university's shortened name) president since 1977, this public university in Columbia, South Carolina, has begun to take its educational mission very seriously indeed. It has developed an extremely ambitious plan to improve itself that, aptly enough, carries an extremely ambitious title: "The 2001 Vision." (You can get a pamphlet outlining the plan called "2001: The New Dimension.") You see, "2001" refers not to the classic movie but to the year of the university's two hundredth birthday. Holderman's primary goal by then – and it's just the main one of many – is to upgrade the university to the point where it will rank among the top ten systems of higher education in the country. Hell, if you're going to bother coming up with a plan at all, might as well set your sights high.

Student reaction to Holderman and "The 2001 Vision" runs the gamut from nearly total ignorance (as in "the 2001 what?") to hearty approval. There are, of course, some grumblings. Plans such as his take lots of money, some of which is necessarily gleaned from tuition hikes, which naturally generates some amount of dissatisfaction. But even the most nominally informed have to notice what Holderman has already accomplished. Students say, "academic quality improves on a daily basis," and they mean it.

Thus far, under "The 2001 Vision," the president has increased the university's private endowment (substantially, even incredibly), raised enrollment standards, increased research and research grants, and improved the quality of the faculty. "This school is much more respected than it once was," which has to feel good to those enrolled. Students call Holderman "a brilliant leader with a vision," joking that he's "stupid enough to try to make Carolina an academically strong school." Although dissenters claim he hasn't done much for the university's people, urging him to curb tuition hikes and to increase low staff and faculty salaries, "on the whole, students are very supportive." ...

– Courtesy of Lisa Birnbach,
New & Improved College Book,
Published in 1990

Index

G

H

I

J

K

L

M

N

O